Survey of Sexual Violence in Adult Correctional Facilities, 2009–11 - Statistical Tables

Ramona R. Rantala, *BJS Statistician*, Jessica Rexroat, *BJS Intern*, and Allen J. Beck, Ph.D., *BJS Statistician*

In 2011, correctional administrators reported 6,660 allegations of sexual victimization in prisons. Of these, 605 were substantiated based on follow-up investigation. Local jail authorities reported 2,042 allegations, of which 284 were substantiated. About half (51%) involved allegations of nonconsensual sexual acts or abusive sexual contacts of inmates with other inmates, and half (49%) involved staff sexual misconduct or sexual harassment directed toward inmates. While the overall number of allegations reported by authorities in adult correctional facilities rose from an estimated 6,241 in 2005 to 8,763 in 2011, the number of substantiated incidents did not change significantly from 2005 (885) to 2011 (902).

Data are from the Bureau of Justice Statistics' (BJS) Survey of Sexual Violence (SSV), which has annually collected official records on allegations and substantiated incidents of inmate-on-inmate and staff-on-inmate sexual victimization since 2004. The SSV is one of a number of BJS data collections that are conducted to meet the mandates of the Prison Rape Elimination Act of 2003 (PREA).

On behalf of BJS, staff of the U.S. Census Bureau mailed survey forms to correctional administrators in the Federal Bureau of Prisons, state prison systems, public and private jails, private prisons, jails in Indian country, and facilities operated by the U.S. military and Immigration and Customs Enforcement (ICE).

Administrators were given the option of mailing back a completed form or completing it on the internet. Data collection forms can be accessed on the BJS website. The administrators then completed a separate form for each substantiated incident, providing details about the victim, perpetrator, and circumstances surrounding the incident.

The 2009, 2010, and 2011 surveys included all federal and state prisons, facilities operated by the U.S. military and ICE, and a representative sample of jail jurisdictions, privately operated jails and prisons, and jails holding adults in Indian country. In total, data were collected from facilities containing 1.99 million inmates in 2009, 1.98 million inmates in 2010, and 1.97 million inmates in 2011. (See *Methodology* for more information about the systems and facilities from which data were collected.)

The statistical tables that follow provide counts of allegations and substantiated incidents by type of victimization for every jurisdiction and facility in the 2009, 2010, 2011 surveys. These tables accompany BJS report, *Sexual Victimization Reported by Adult Correctional Authorities, 2009–11*, NCJ 234904, which provides national estimates and rates of sexual victimization as well as an in-depth examination of substantiated incidents covering the number and characteristics of victims and perpetrators, location, time of day, nature of the injuries, impact on the victims, and sanctions imposed on the perpetrators.

Defining sexual victimization

To define sexual victimization under the Prison Rape Elimination Act of 2003, BJS uses uniform definitions that classify each sexual act by the perpetrator who carried out it (i.e., inmate or staff) and the type of act.

Inmate-on-inmate sexual victimization involves sexual contact with a victim without his or her consent or with a victim who cannot consent or refuse.

Nonconsensual sexual acts are the most serious victimizations, and include—

- contact between the penis and the vagina or the penis and the anus including penetration, however slight

- contact between the mouth and the penis, vagina, or anus

- penetration of the anal or genital opening of another person by a hand, finger, or other object.

Abusive sexual contacts are less serious victimizations, and include—

- intentional touching, either directly or through clothing, of the genitalia, anus, groin, breast, inner thigh, or buttocks of any person

- incidents in which the intent was to sexually exploit (rather than to harm or debilitate).

Staff-on-inmate sexual victimization includes both consensual and nonconsensual acts perpetrated on an inmate by staff. Staff includes an employee, volunteer, contractor, official visitor, or other agency representative. Family, friends, and other visitors are excluded.

Staff sexual misconduct includes any act or behavior of a sexual nature directed toward an inmate by staff, including romantic relationships. Such acts include—

- intentional touching of the genitalia, anus, groin, breast, inner thigh, or buttocks with the intent to abuse, arouse, or gratify sexual desire

- completed, attempted, threatened, or requested sexual acts

- occurrences of indecent exposure, invasion of privacy, or staff voyeurism for sexual gratification.

Staff sexual harassment includes repeated verbal statements or comments of a sexual nature to an inmate by staff. Such statements include—

- demeaning references to an inmate's sex or derogatory comments about his or her body or clothing

- repeated profane or obscene language or gestures.

Methodology

Sampling

The sampling designs for the Bureau of Justice Statistics' (BJS) 2009, 2010, and 2011 Survey of Sexual Violence (SSV) varied according to the different facilities covered under PREA.

Federal and state prisons

In each year, the survey included the Federal Bureau of Prisons and all 50 state adult prison systems. Prison administrators were directed to report only on allegations of sexual victimization that occurred within publicly operated adult prison facilities and to exclude allegations involving inmates held in local jails, privately operated facilities, and facilities in other jurisdictions.

Privately operated state and federal prisons

In each year, a sample of 125 privately operated state and federal prison facilities was drawn to produce a sample of the private prisons identified by the 2005 Census of State and Federal Adult Correctional Facilities. The sampling frame of privately operated prison facilities contained 417 facilities in 2009 and 2010 and 393 in 2011 (after removing prisons that had closed). Facilities were sorted by average daily population (ADP) in the 12-month period ending June 30, 2005. In 2009 and 2010, 71 facilities with ADPs of 488 or more were selected with certainty because of their size. In 2011, 69 facilities with ADPs of 445 or more were selected with certainty (i.e., given a 100% chance of selection in each sample because of their size).

The remaining facilities were sorted by region (i.e., the Northeast, Midwest, South, or West), state, and ADP, and sampled systematically with probabilities proportional to their size. Fifty-four facilities were selected in 2009 and 2010, and 56 in 2011.[1]

Among the privately operated prisons selected for the survey, 3 had closed prior to data collection in 2009, 14 in 2010, and 10 in 2011. Three facilities selected in 2009 were out-of-scope. Six privately operated prisons did not respond to the survey in 2009:

- Carver Correctional Center, Oklahoma City, OK

- Crossroads Adult Transitional Center, Chicago, IL

- Dismas Charities, El Paso, TX

- Dismas House, St. Louis, MO

- Joseph Coleman Center, Philadelphia, PA

- Stepping Stones (Community Alcohol Drug Center), Mitchell, SD.

All selected and active privately operated prisons in 2010 and 2011 participated in the survey.

Public jails

In each year, 700 publicly operated jail facilities were selected based on data reported in BJS's Deaths in Custody Reporting Program (DCRP). Based on the DCRP data in each year prior to the survey, the largest jail jurisdiction was selected in 45 states and the District of Columbia.[2]

Jail jurisdictions with ADPs greater than or equal to 1,000 inmates were also selected with certainty (128 in 2009, 131 in 2010, and 117 in 2011). The remaining jail jurisdictions on the frame were then grouped into three strata.

- In the 2009 sample, 99 jails (out of 1,489) with an ADP of 85 or fewer inmates were selected in the first stratum, 317 jails (out of 770) with an ADP of 86 to 268 inmates were selected from the second stratum, and 110 jails (out of 434) with an ADP of 269 to 999 inmates were selected from the third stratum.

- In the 2010 sample, 117 jails (out of 1,476) with an ADP of 85 or fewer inmates were selected in the first stratum; 247 jails (out of 762) with an ADP of 86 to 267 inmates were selected from the second stratum; and 159 jails (out of 436) with an ADP of 268 to 999 inmates were selected from the third stratum.

- In the 2011 sample, 197 jails (out of 1,489) with an ADP of 87 or fewer inmates were selected in the first stratum, 120 jails (out of 773) with an ADP of 88 to 273 inmates were selected from the second stratum, and 220 jails (out of 427) with an ADP of 274 to 999 inmates were selected from the third stratum.

During the three years, only one publicly operated jail closed prior to data collection (in 2009). Among the remaining selected jail jurisdictions in 2009, six did not respond to the survey:

- Bessemer City Jail, Bessemer, AL

- Cooke County Justice Center, Gainesville, TX

- Marshall County Jail, Marshalltown, IA

- Oklahoma County Jail, Oklahoma City, OK

- Osage County Jail, Linn, MO

- Roberts County Jail, Sisseton, SD.

---

[1]The chance that a facility would be selected was directly related to the size of the facility (i.e., within each stratum, facilities with larger ADPs had a greater chance being selected than facilities with smaller ADPs).

[2]Five states with combined jail-prison systems had no public jails: Connecticut, Delaware, Hawaii, Rhode Island, and Vermont.

Among the 700 jail jurisdictions selected in 2010, 8 did not respond to the survey:

- Cumberland County Sheriff's Office, Portland, ME

- Erie County Holding Center, Buffalo, NY

- Houston County Sheriff's Office, Dotham, AL

- Morgan County Sheriff's Office, Decatur, AL

- Pottawatomie County Sheriff's Office, Shawnee, OK

- Ray County Sheriff's Office, Henrietta, MO

- St. Louis Department of Public Safety, St. Louis, MO

- Wichita Falls County Sheriff's Office, Wichita Falls, TX.

Among the 700 selected in 2011, 4 did not respond to the survey:

- Cumberland County Sheriff's Office, Portland, ME

- Ostego County Jail, Gaylord, MI

- Tazewell County Jail, Pekin, IL

- Victoria County Jail, Victoria, TX.

Private jails

In each year, a sample of 15 privately operated jails was selected based on data reported in the DCRP files. The DCRP file listed 41 privately operated jails in 2008, 38 in 2009, and 34 in 2010. The facilities on the sampling frame were sorted by region, state, and ADP. Based on their large ADP, two facilities were selected with certainty in 2009, three in 2010, and four in 2011. The remaining private jails in each year were systematically sampled with probabilities proportional to size.

Among the sampled facilities, one had closed prior to data collection in 2009 and one had closed in 2010. All selected and active privately operated jails in 2009, 2010, and 2011 participated in the survey.

Other correctional facilities

A sample of 15 adult jails in Indian country was selected each year. Based on BJS's Jails in Indian Country collection program, jails that held adults only or adults and juveniles were eligible for the sampling frame. Jails that held only juveniles were included in the juvenile SSV data collection.

Each year the sample was selected through probabilities proportionate to size, with ADP as the measure of size. For sampling purposes, jails with an ADP of less than one inmate, were assigned 1 as their measure of size. Due to their relatively large size, two jails were selected with certainty in 2009, three in 2010, and three in 2011. There were 63 adult

jails in Indian country in 2009, 61 in 2010, and 59 in 2011. The remaining jails were sorted by state and ADP and then selected with probability proportionate to size.

Of the adult jails selected in Indian country from 2009 through 2011, one closed prior to data collection:

- Truxton Canyon Adult Detention Center, AZ (closed in 2010).

Five Indian country jails did not respond to the survey:

- Choctaw Justice Complex Adult Division, MS (2011)

- Fort Peck Police Department and Adult Detention, MT (2009)

- Oglala Sioux Tribal Offenders Facility, SD (2010 and 2011)

- Rosebud Sioux Tribal Police Department and Adult Detention, SD (2009)

- Standing Rock Law Enforcement and Adult Detention Center, ND (2011).

Two additional censuses of other correctional facilities were conducted to represent—

- all facilities operated by the U.S. Air Force, U.S. Army, U.S. Navy, and the U.S. Marine Corps in the continental United States

- all facilities operated by or exclusively for Immigration and Customs Enforcement (ICE) were selected.[3]

All of the facilities under active operation by the U.S. military and Immigration and Customs Enforcement (ICE) participated the 2009, 2010, and 2011 surveys.

Reports of sexual victimization

Since BJS first developed uniform definitions of sexual victimization, correctional administrators have significantly enhanced their abilities to report uniform data on sexual victimization. In 2011, administrators in 47 state prison systems reported allegations of abusive sexual contacts separately from nonconsensual sexual acts, an increase of 5 systems since 2006. One state limited counts of nonconsensual sexual acts to completed (versus attempted and completed) acts. The majority of state prison systems reported data on staff sexual misconduct using survey definitions. Four systems were unable to separate staff sexual harassment from misconduct, and one system did not track allegations of staff sexual harassment in a central database.

---

[3]Based on information from the ICE integrated decision support system, 19 facilities were operating in 2009 and 2010, and 18 facilities in 2011. In 2011, Willacy Detention Center, TX, no longer operated as an ICE facility.

Public jail administrators were less likely than prison administrators to report sexual victimization based on the definitions provided. More than a quarter (27%) of the 695 public jail jurisdictions selected in 2011 did not record abusive sexual contacts separately from the more serious nonconsensual sexual acts in 2008. This is an improvement over the 2006 SSV, in which a third (36%) of public jail jurisdictions did not record this information. Ten public jail jurisdictions did not record allegations of abusive sexual contacts, 10 based counts of nonconsensual sexual acts on completed acts only, and 22 based counts of nonconsensual sexual acts on substantiated incidents only. Finally, four public jail jurisdictions did not keep records on allegations of nonconsensual sexual acts.

Most public jail administrators reported staff sexual victimization based on the SSV definitions. However, 19% could not separate allegations of staff sexual harassment from allegations of staff sexual misconduct. Three did not record allegations of staff sexual misconduct, while 19 recorded substantiated incidents only. Seven did not record allegations of staff sexual harassment.

List of tables

Section 1. Federal and state prisons

Section 2. Public local jails

Section 3. Privately operated prisons and jails

Section 4. Other correctional facilities: U.S. military, U.S. Immigration and Customs Enforcement, and Jails in Indian Country

Section 1: Federal and state prisons

TABLE 1
Allegations of sexual victimization reported by federal and state prison authorities, by type of victimization, 2011

Jurisdiction and facility	Prisoners in custody on 12/31/2011[a]	Inmate-on-inmate				Staff-on-inmate			
		Nonconsensual sexual acts		Abusive sexual contact		Sexual misconduct		Sexual harassment	
		Alleged	Substantiated	Alleged	Substantiated	Alleged	Substantiated	Alleged	Substantiated
Total	1,373,194	2,002	133	1,028	161	1,992	207	1,231	45
Federal	176,228	77	3	42	1	230	3	139	2
State	1,196,966	1,925	130	986	160	1,762	204	1,092	43
Alabama	26,268	27	4	17	2	32	12	12	1
Alaska	3,708	9	4	4	1	1	0	0	0
Arizona[b]	33,492	48	3	21	2	53	4	/	/
Arkansas	14,090	3	1	11	5	9	4	5	1
California	146,881	104	2	38	1	54	0	5	0
Colorado	17,559	16	2	18	3	42	8	7	0
Connecticut	17,022	16	0	19	3	4	0	0	0
Delaware	6,546	28	5	19	1	8	2	5	1
Florida	89,034	223	1	57	1	169	4	374	1
Georgia[c]	47,229	69	1	/	/	33	4	10	0
Hawaii	3,687	4	1	0	0	2	0	1	0
Idaho[b,c]	5,138	5	3	/	/	4	0	/	/
Illinois	48,427	25	2	7	2	18	2	0	0
Indiana	24,450	23	1	21	7	17	5	5	3
Iowa	9,115	24	2	64	21	47	16	10	0
Kansas	9,256	81	4	26	2	43	2	22	1
Kentucky	11,951	22	2	15	2	21	3	2	0
Louisiana	15,893	14	2	2	0	25	3	11	0
Maine	1,978	8	0	3	0	4	0	0	0
Maryland[b,c]	22,923	13	0	/	/	17	0	/	/
Massachusetts	11,467	29	0	19	1	18	1	2	0
Michigan	42,904	33	5	27	9	24	7	307	4
Minnesota[d]	9,309	21	0	10	0	8	1	0	0
Mississippi	10,721	13	0	1	0	5	3	0	0
Missouri	30,969	74	14	29	3	117	6	64	7
Montana	1,707	9	3	2	0	9	1	2	0
Nebraska	4,657	29	1	17	2	39	3	28	2
Nevada	12,159	33	3	9	0	18	3	20	0
New Hampshire	2,423	4	1	14	0	6	0	0	0
New Jersey	20,755	8	0	1	1	5	1	1	0
New Mexico	3,834	6	1	0	0	2	0	0	0
New York	55,196	60	5	14	3	184	4	24	2
North Carolina	39,632	42	1	27	7	137	19	72	6
North Dakota	1,385	3	1	1	0	1	0	2	0
Ohio	47,957	64	8	30	11	46	8	5	0
Oklahoma	17,724	26	1	32	5	23	10	6	2
Oregon	13,728	21	0	13	3	14	0	3	2
Pennsylvania	48,515	30	2	6	3	49	5	16	0
Rhode Island	3,032	7	1	6	4	4	1	0	0
South Carolina	22,343	0	0	0	0	2	2	0	0
South Dakota	3,551	2	1	4	0	2	1	0	0
Tennessee[b]	14,684	20	0	22	3	21	2	16	0
Texas[e]	141,353	393	8	195	9	109	12	/	/
Utah	5,294	10	3	18	3	7	4	0	0
Vermont	1,531	14	8	17	9	20	7	3	2
Virginia	28,962	16	0	18	3	21	9	5	0
Washington	17,109	134	6	62	9	221	15	31	3

TABLE 1 (continued)
Allegations of sexual victimization reported by federal and state prison authorities, by type of victimization, 2011

| Jurisdiction and facility | Prisoners in custody on 12/31/2011[a] | Inmate-on-inmate | | | | Staff-on-inmate | | | |
| | | Nonconsensual sexual acts | | Abusive sexual contact | | Sexual misconduct | | Sexual harassment | |
		Alleged	Substantiated	Alleged	Substantiated	Alleged	Substantiated	Alleged	Substantiated
West Virginia	5,149	12	2	14	6	14	2	7	1
Wisconsin	22,352	44	12	17	7	28	6	5	1
Wyoming	1,917	6	3	19	6	5	2	4	3

/ Not reported.

[a]Excludes inmates in privately operated facilities and facilities operated and administered by local governments. Counts were based on National Prisoner Statistics, 2011, "Inmates in custody of state or federal correctional facilities, excluding private prisons, December 31, 1978–2011," generated using the Corrections Statistical Analysis Tool at www.bjs.gov.

[b]Allegations of staff sexual harassment could not be counted separately from staff sexual misconduct.

[c]Allegations of abusive sexual contact could not be counted separately from allegations of nonconsensual sexual acts.

[d]Counts of nonconsensual sexual acts were based on completed acts only.

[e]Agency did not record allegations of staff sexual harassment.

Source: Bureau of Justice Statistics, Survey of Sexual Violence, 2011.

TABLE 2
Allegations of sexual victimization reported by federal and state prison authorities, by type of victimization, 2010

Jurisdiction and facility	Prisoners in custody on 12/31/2010[a]	Inmate-on-inmate				Staff-on-inmate			
		Nonconsensual sexual acts		Abusive sexual contact		Sexual misconduct		Sexual harassment	
		Alleged	Substantiated	Alleged	Substantiated	Alleged	Substantiated	Alleged	Substantiated
Total	1,393,468	1,873	113	984	163	2,014	216	1,420	65
Federal	173,138	81	1	34	2	230	7	134	6
State	1,220,330	1,792	112	950	161	1,784	209	1,286	59
Alabama	26,321	20	4	29	12	23	5	9	2
Alaska	3,771	5	0	0	0	1	0	0	0
Arizona[b]	34,774	52	4	15	0	43	5	/	/
Arkansas	14,192	0	0	8	3	32	13	12	4
California	160,651	96	5	32	5	36	3	8	0
Colorado	18,254	22	3	26	4	44	8	7	1
Connecticut	17,746	19	1	14	1	5	0	0	0
Delaware	6,378	10	0	3	0	4	0	2	0
Florida	90,274	268	1	58	0	193	2	408	0
Georgia[c]	47,561	90	6	/	/	42	5	8	0
Hawaii	3,363	1	0	0	0	0	0	1	1
Idaho[d]	4,999	2	2	1	0	2	0	0	0
Illinois	48,418	24	2	2	0	18	2	3	0
Indiana	24,456	23	1	16	4	20	8	11	5
Iowa	9,457	28	5	32	10	49	11	8	0
Kansas	9,055	31	0	33	2	54	3	24	0
Kentucky	12,374	18	2	13	4	26	4	1	0
Louisiana	16,087	11	3	4	1	50	3	37	0
Maine[c]	1,954	5	3	/	/	2	1	1	0
Maryland[b,c]	22,786	22	1	/	/	16	1	/	/
Massachusetts	11,162	26	5	29	8	20	1	2	0
Michigan[e]	44,113	22	6	25	10	13	5	275	3
Minnesota	9,397	30	1	1	0	10	3	0	0
Mississippi	11,213	6	0	0	0	12	6	0	0
Missouri	30,577	60	5	14	2	74	1	27	1
Montana	1,635	9	1	4	2	9	0	2	0
Nebraska	4,608	24	2	16	1	20	1	27	6
Nevada	12,192	16	2	16	6	26	1	13	1
New Hampshire	2,617	12	1	2	0	9	0	1	0
New Jersey	21,647	9	0	0	0	8	5	1	0
New Mexico	3,754	3	2	1	1	3	1	0	0
New York	56,420	47	2	14	3	168	8	65	3
North Carolina	40,167	47	1	33	8	212	17	149	9
North Dakota	1,416	0	0	2	2	0	0	0	0
Ohio	48,671	49	5	33	13	30	9	11	0
Oklahoma	18,128	23	3	12	4	13	7	6	3
Oregon	13,859	25	1	9	2	12	1	5	3
Pennsylvania[f]	47,072	27	0	2	2	20	3	/	/
Rhode Island	3,159	5	1	5	1	3	0	0	0
South Carolina[d]	22,992	2	2	0	0	6	6	0	0
South Dakota	3,388	2	0	2	1	1	1	0	0
Tennessee	14,917	16	2	10	1	33	13	13	0
Texas[f]	141,087	331	0	264	9	47	2	/	/
Utah	5,442	5	1	37	3	1	0	1	0
Vermont	1,517	12	4	19	15	13	2	8	3
Virginia	30,351	24	1	12	3	35	7	13	0
Washington	17,028	154	5	70	9	259	25	121	12

TABLE 2 (continued)
Allegations of sexual victimization reported by federal and state prison authorities, by type of victimization, 2010

	Prisoners in custody on 12/31/2010[a]	Inmate-on-inmate				Staff-on-inmate			
		Nonconsensual sexual acts		Abusive sexual contact		Sexual misconduct		Sexual harassment	
Jurisdiction and facility		Alleged	Substantiated	Alleged	Substantiated	Alleged	Substantiated	Alleged	Substantiated
West Virginia	5,072	4	3	9	2	34	4	2	1
Wisconsin	21,983	46	6	7	2	28	5	3	1
Wyoming	1,875	9	7	16	5	5	1	1	0

/ Not reported.

[a]Excludes inmates in privately operated facilities and facilities operated and administered by local governments. Counts were based on National Prisoner Statistics, 2010, "Inmates in custody of state or federal correctional facilities, excluding private prisons, December 31, 1978–2011," generated using the Corrections Statistical Analysis Tool at www.bjs.gov.

[b]Allegations of staff sexual harassment could not be counted separately from staff sexual misconduct.

[c]Allegations of abusive sexual contact could not be counted separately from allegations of nonconsensual sexual acts.

[d]Counts of nonconsensual sexual acts were based on substantiated acts only.

[e]Counts of nonconsensual sexual acts were based on completed acts only.

[f]Agency did not record allegations of staff sexual harassment.

Source: Bureau of Justice Statistics, Survey of Sexual Violence, 2010.

TABLE 3
Allegations of sexual victimization reported by federal and state prison authorities, by type of victimization, 2009

Jurisdiction and facility	Prisoners in custody on 12/31/2009[a]	Inmate-on-inmate				Staff-on-inmate			
		Nonconsensual sexual acts		Abusive sexual contact		Sexual misconduct		Sexual harassment	
		Alleged	Substantiated	Alleged	Substantiated	Alleged	Substantiated	Alleged	Substantiated
Total	1,395,317	1,379	101	1,270	153	2,057	218	1,391	46
Federal	171,000	58	0	28	0	197	2	122	6
State	1,224,317	1,321	101	1,242	153	1,860	216	1,269	40
Alabama	26,358	57	2	5	1	29	4	1	0
Alaska	3,846	4	1	1	0	0	0	0	0
Arizona	31,573	38	1	14	0	41	5	0	0
Arkansas	13,338	15	5	16	5	44	2	14	0
California	166,514	95	2	44	2	33	2	1	0
Colorado	17,768	22	2	8	3	10	3	14	1
Connecticut	18,053	15	1	15	1	5	1	1	0
Delaware	6,581	9	0	5	0	5	1	0	0
Florida	91,561	50	0	221	0	161	3	372	3
Georgia[b,c]	48,409	38	0	/	/	34	2	27	1
Hawaii[c]	3,200	1	1	/	/	0	0	1	0
Idaho[c,d,e]	5,118	1	1	/	/	5	3	/	/
Illinois	45,161	25	4	10	0	26	5	1	0
Indiana	24,269	30	0	16	3	51	12	9	2
Iowa	8,914	31	5	51	18	48	11	14	2
Kansas	8,644	26	4	24	4	31	1	11	1
Kentucky	12,493	23	2	8	1	13	2	2	0
Louisiana	16,967	19	3	4	2	70	2	77	0
Maine	2,074	1	1	3	2	3	2	1	1
Maryland[c]	21,962	23	0	/	/	2	1	20	0
Massachusetts	11,156	30	7	25	6	29	3	4	0
Michigan[b]	45,478	8	4	32	13	31	2	357	1
Minnesota	9,309	23	5	5	1	12	0	0	0
Mississippi[c,e]	11,926	4	0	/	/	1	1	/	/
Missouri	30,519	56	7	8	2	128	12	11	3
Montana	1,651	25	6	7	5	25	0	2	0
Nebraska	4,490	9	0	17	2	27	0	20	1
Nevada	12,570	12	2	5	1	14	1	8	0
New Hampshire	2,915	7	0	3	0	8	0	0	0
New Jersey	21,165	5	0	0	0	5	3	1	0
New Mexico	3,762	3	1	0	0	3	0	3	1
New York	58,479	33	1	7	0	173	12	38	2
North Carolina	39,916	54	1	24	10	230	23	125	3
North Dakota	1,436	1	0	2	2	1	0	2	0
Ohio	48,588	57	10	25	10	41	8	10	0
Oklahoma	18,064	40	3	11	4	34	9	6	2
Oregon	13,735	15	1	7	1	10	2	5	0
Pennsylvania	49,565	26	5	13	4	21	6	13	1
Rhode Island[e]	3,413	3	0	3	2	7	2	/	/
South Carolina[d]	23,671	1	1	1	1	2	2	0	0
South Dakota	3,377	13	0	9	0	5	3	0	0
Tennessee	14,824	26	0	3	1	14	6	4	0
Texas[f]	139,335	168	0	450	5	73	3	/	/
Utah	5,244	12	2	28	2	6	1	1	1
Vermont	1,552	16	2	27	14	26	12	7	2
Virginia	29,420	30	2	8	3	34	13	2	2
Washington	17,131	84	4	35	9	211	17	62	8

TABLE 3 (continued)

Allegations of sexual victimization reported by federal and state prison authorities, by type of victimization, 2009

Jurisdiction and facility	Prisoners in custody on 12/31/2009[a]	Inmate-on-inmate				Staff-on-inmate			
		Nonconsensual sexual acts		Abusive sexual contact		Sexual misconduct		Sexual harassment	
		Alleged	Substantiated	Alleged	Substantiated	Alleged	Substantiated	Alleged	Substantiated
West Virginia	5,062	4	0	1	1	25	11	6	2
Wisconsin	22,245	33	2	36	9	49	1	16	0
Wyoming	1,516	0	0	5	3	4	1	0	0

/ Not reported.

[a]Excludes inmates in privately operated facilities and facilities operated and administered by local governments. Counts were based on National Prisoner Statistics, 2009, "Inmates in custody of state or federal correctional facilities, excluding private prisons, December 31, 1978–2011," generated using the Corrections Statistical Analysis Tool at www.bjs.gov.

[b]Counts of nonconsensual sexual acts were based on completed acts only.

[c]Allegations of abusive sexual contact could not be counted separately from allegations of nonconsensual sexual acts.

[d]Counts of nonconsensual sexual acts were based on substantiated acts only.

[e]Allegations of staff sexual harassment could not be counted separately from staff sexual misconduct.

[f]Agency did not record allegations of staff sexual harassment.

Source: Bureau of Justice Statistics, Survey of Sexual Violence, 2009.

Section 2. Public local jails

TABLE 4
Allegations of sexual victimization reported by local jail authorities, by type of victimization, 2011

Jurisdiction and facility	Average daily population	Inmate-on-inmate				Staff-on-inmate			
		Nonconsensual sexual acts		Abusive sexual contact		Sexual misconduct		Sexual harassment	
		Alleged	Substantiated	Alleged	Substantiated	Alleged	Substantiated	Alleged	Substantiated
Total	347,083	615	54	244	42	390	48	98	19
Alabama									
Jefferson Co.[a,b]	1,127	3	1	/	/	0	0	/	/
Madison Co.	935	0	0	1	0	0	0	0	0
Mobile Co.[a,b]	1,560	2	0	/	/	0	0	/	/
Morgan Co.[a,b]	266	1	0	/	/	1	1	/	/
Russellville City[a,b]	6	0	0	/	/	1	1	/	/
Shelby Co.[c]	410	0	0	0	0	1	1	0	0
Winston Co.	60	0	0	0	0	1	0	0	0
Arizona									
Coconino Co.	509	0	0	0	0	1	0	0	0
Maricopa Co.[a]	7,358	17	0	/	/	8	0	5	0
Pima Co.	1,661	8	0	0	0	0	0	0	0
Yuma Co.	605	0	0	0	0	0	0	12	0
Arkansas									
Faulkner Co.	341	0	0	0	0	1	0	1	0
Miller Co.	222	2	0	0	0	0	0	0	0
California									
Alameda Co.	3,755	1	1	3	0	0	0	1	0
Amador Co.	78	1	1	0	0	0	0	0	0
Fresno Co.	2,246	4	0	1	0	1	0	0	0
Imperial Co.	568	0	0	0	0	1	0	0	0
Kern Co.	2,427	1	0	0	0	2	2	1	1
Los Angeles Co.[a,d]	15,766	11	0	/	/	6	0	/	/
Orange Co.	5,805	1	0	1	0	3	2	0	0
Placer Co.[a,e]	551	1	0	/	/	0	0	0	0
Riverside Co.	3,264	3	1	2	2	1	0	0	0
Sacramento Co.	2,134	4	0	1	0	0	0	0	0
San Bernardino Co. West Valley Det. Ctr.	5,507	7	7	0	0	0	0	0	0
San Diego Co.[a]	4,630	12	0	/	/	1	0	0	0
San Francisco Co. & City[a]	1,564	1	0	/	/	3	0	0	0
San Joaquin Co.[b]	1,203	1	0	3	1	1	1	/	/
Santa Barbara Co.	899	0	0	0	0	2	0	0	0
Santa Clara Co.	3,562	5	0	2	0	0	0	0	0
Stanislaus Co.[a]	1,020	0	0	/	/	1	0	0	0
Tulare Co.	1,374	2	1	0	0	1	1	0	0
Colorado									
Adams Co. Det. Fac.	1,098	0	0	1	1	1	0	0	0
Arapahoe Co.	1,198	1	1	2	0	1	0	0	0
Bent Co.	2	1	1	0	0	1	1	0	0
Boulder Co.	445	0	0	4	1	0	0	0	0
Denver Co.[b]	2,104	0	0	9	0	2	0	/	/
Douglas Co.	338	0	0	1	1	0	0	0	0
El Paso Co.	1,264	0	0	1	1	2	1	0	0
Jefferson Co.[b]	1,139	2	1	3	0	0	0	/	/
Pueblo Co.	535	1	1	0	0	1	0	0	0
District of Columbia									
District of Columbia[a,b]	2,107	2	1	/	/	0	0	/	/

TABLE 4 (continued)
Allegations of sexual victimization reported by local jail authorities, by type of victimization, 2011

| | | Inmate-on-inmate | | | | Staff-on-inmate | | | |
| | Average daily | Nonconsensual sexual acts | | Abusive sexual contact | | Sexual misconduct | | Sexual harassment | |
Jurisdiction and facility	population	Alleged	Substantiated	Alleged	Substantiated	Alleged	Substantiated	Alleged	Substantiated
Florida									
Brevard Co.	1,579	1	0	1	0	0	0	0	0
Broward Co. Det. Ctr.	4,450	3	0	0	0	5	1	0	0
Indian River Co.	509	4	0	0	0	3	1	1	0
Jacksonville City	3,986	5	0	1	1	0	0	0	0
Lee Co.	1,718	1	0	1	0	1	0	0	0
Manatee Co.	1,048	1	0	1	0	0	0	0	0
Marion Co.[a,b]	1,668	4	1	/	/	0	0	/	/
Miami-Dade Co. Corr. & Rehab	5,418	8	0	1	0	7	0	3	0
Orange Co.	3,403	2	0	4	2	1	1	1	1
Palm Beach Co.	2,502	4	0	0	0	2	0	0	0
Pasco Co.[b]	1,356	1	0	0	0	0	0	0	0
Pinellas Co.	3,084	2	0	0	0	0	0	0	0
Polk Co.	2,109	6	0	10	1	1	0	0	0
Santa Rosa Co.	497	0	0	0	0	1	0	0	0
Seminole Co. John E. Polk Corr. Fac.	930	1	0	0	0	0	0	0	0
St. Lucie Co.	1,206	0	0	3	2	1	0	0	0
Volusia Co. Division of Corr.	1,400	2	0	0	0	1	0	0	0
Georgia									
Atlanta City Det. Ctr.[a,b]	481	11	5	/	/	4	0	/	/
Carroll Co.	514	1	0	0	0	0	0	0	0
Chatham Co.[a]	1,745	2	0	/	/	1	0	1	0
Clayton Co.[a]	1,724	1	0	/	/	0	0	1	0
Cobb Co. Jail & Prison[a,b]	2,258	1	0	/	/	0	0	/	/
Decatur Co. Prison	295	2	0	0	0	0	0	0	0
Dekalb Co.[a]	3,376	1	0	/	/	0	0	0	0
Dougherty Co.	916	1	0	0	0	0	0	0	0
Fayette Co.[a]	292	4	1	/	/	0	0	1	1
Floyd Co.[a]	681	2	0	/	/	0	0	0	0
Fulton Co.[a,c]	3,052	3	0	/	/	0	0	/	/
Gwinnett Co. Det. Ctr.	2,590	0	0	0	0	1	0	0	0
Laurens Co.[a]	245	0	0	/	/	2	0	2	0
Muscogee Co.	1,140	3	1	1	0	0	0	1	0
Newton Co.[a,b]	665	0	0	/	/	1	1	/	/
Troup Co. Jail	423	1	0	0	0	0	0	0	0
Idaho									
Canyon Co.	393	0	0	2	0	1	0	0	0
Illinois									
Cook Co.	9,974	20	2	5	0	3	0	0	0
Kane Co.	618	0	0	1	0	0	0	0	0
Kankakee Co.[a]	650	1	0	/	/	1	0	0	0
Logan Co.[a,b]	31	1	0	/	/	0	0	/	/
Indiana									
Allen Co.	840	1	0	0	0	0	0	0	0
Clark Co.	460	2	1	0	0	1	1	0	0
Elkhart Co.[a]	867	3	1	/	/	1	0	0	0
Gibson Co.	119	0	0	0	0	0	0	1	1
Marion Co.	1,090	2	0	0	0	1	1	0	0
Vanderburgh Co.	537	2	1	0	0	0	0	0	0
Wayne Co.	283	0	0	0	0	1	0	0	0
Iowa									
Polk Co.	909	27	0	0	0	3	0	0	0

TABLE 4 (continued)
Allegations of sexual victimization reported by local jail authorities, by type of victimization, 2011

Jurisdiction and facility	Average daily population	Inmate-on-inmate				Staff-on-inmate			
		Nonconsensual sexual acts		Abusive sexual contact		Sexual misconduct		Sexual harassment	
		Alleged	Substantiated	Alleged	Substantiated	Alleged	Substantiated	Alleged	Substantiated
Kansas									
Greenwood Co.	22	0	0	0	0	1	0	0	0
Sedgwick Co. Det. Ctr.[a]	1,502	4	0	/	/	1	0	0	0
Wyandotte Co.[a,b]	330	1	0	/	/	2	0	/	/
Kentucky									
Daviess Co. Det. Ctr.[a]	601	0	0	/	/	0	0	1	/
Fayette Co. Det. Ctr.	1,163	0	0	0	0	6	0	0	0
Fulton Co. Det. Ctr.[a,b]	350	2	0	/	/	0	0	/	/
Henderson Co. Det. Ctr.	550	1	1	1	1	1	0	0	0
Hopkins Co.	407	0	0	0	0	4	0	0	0
Louisville Metropolitan[a]	1,991	7	1	/	/	5	0	0	0
Louisiana									
Caddo Parish Corr. Ctr.	1,279	3	0	0	0	0	0	0	0
Calvasieu Parish Corr. Ctr.	1,251	4	0	0	0	0	0	0	0
Claiborne Parish Det. Fac.	577	1	0	1	0	0	0	0	0
Franklin Parish Det. Ctr.[a]	794	4	0	/	/	0	0	1	0
Jackson Parish Corr. Ctr.[b]	1,097	1	0	2	0	0	0	/	/
Jefferson Parish	956	10	0	1	0	1	0	0	0
Orleans Parish Prison	3,177	6	0	2	1	1	1	0	0
St. Martin Parish[b]	171	2	0	0	0	0	0	/	/
St. Tammany Parish	998	4	1	14	0	1	0	0	0
Sulphur City[a,b]	12	0	0	/	/	1	0	/	/
Terrebone Parish C.J. Complex	673	5	1	0	0	0	0	0	0
West Baton Rouge Parish	274	0	0	1	0	0	0	0	0
Maine									
Waldo Co.	25	1	0	0	0	1	0	0	0
Maryland									
Anne Arundel Co.[a]	856	3	0	/	/	0	0	0	0
Baltimore City Det. Ctr.[a,b]	3,452	2	0	/	/	1	1	/	/
Baltimore Co.	1,368	3	1	5	3	0	0	0	0
Charles Co. Det. Ctr.	455	0	0	1	0	1	0	0	0
Dorchester Co.	167	1	0	0	0	1	0	0	0
Frederick Co.	414	3	0	0	0	0	0	0	0
Montgomery Co. Det. Ctr.	1,001	1	0	1	0	1	0	0	0
Washington Co.[a]	413	3	1	/	/	0	0	0	0
Massachusetts									
Barnstable Co.[a]	418	3	0	/	/	1	0	1	0
Bristol Co.	1,400	10	2	4	1	4	0	0	0
Hampden Co.	1,548	2	0	1	0	3	1	0	0
Suffolk Co.	672	2	0	0	0	0	0	0	0
Suffolk Co. House of Corr.	1,405	1	/	6	/	0	/	0	/
Michigan									
Kent Co.	971	3	0	0	0	0	0	0	0
Manistee Co.[a]	48	0	0	/	/	1	0	0	0
Muskegon Co.	415	1	0	0	0	0	0	2	0
Oakland Co.	360	2	0	0	0	0	0	1	0
Tuscola Co.	85	0	0	0	0	1	0	0	0
Washtenaw Co.	345	0	0	2	1	0	0	0	0
Wayne Co.[a,b]	2,094	6	0	/	/	1	1	/	/
Minnesota									
Hennepin Co. Adult Det. Ctr.[a]	683	2	0	/	/	0	0	0	0
Northwest Reg. Corr. Ctr.	123	1	0	0	0	0	0	0	0
Ramsey Co.	356	2	0	2	0	0	0	0	0
Mississippi									
Harrison Co.[a]	992	2	0	/	/	1	0	0	0

TABLE 4 (continued)
Allegations of sexual victimization reported by local jail authorities, by type of victimization, 2011

| | | Inmate-on-inmate | | | | Staff-on-inmate | | | |
| | | Nonconsensual sexual acts | | Abusive sexual contact | | Sexual misconduct | | Sexual harassment | |
Jurisdiction and facility	Average daily population	Alleged	Substantiated	Alleged	Substantiated	Alleged	Substantiated	Alleged	Substantiated
Missouri									
Adair Co.	37	1	0	0	0	0	0	0	0
Boone Co.[a]	228	1	0	/	/	1	0	0	0
Crawford Co.	90	1	0	0	0	0	0	0	0
Jackson Co. Det. Ctr.	793	0	0	1	0	1	0	0	0
St. Louis City	1,702	0	0	0	0	0	0	2	0
St. Louis Co.	1,291	0	0	0	0	5	2	2	0
Montana									
Dawson Co.[a,b]	164	4	0	/	/	0	0	/	/
Gallatin Co.	74	0	0	0	0	0	0	3	0
Missoula Co.[a,b]	297	3	2	/	/	0	0	/	/
Nebraska									
Douglas Co.[a,b]	1,165	17	0	0	0	4	0	/	/
Gage Co.[b]	26	0	0	1	0	0	0	/	/
Nevada									
Clark Co. Det. Ctr.	3,252	9	2	2	0	5	0	0	0
Washoe Co. Det. Ctr.	993	1	0	0	0	0	0	0	0
New Hampshire									
Strafford Co.[a,b]	431	8	0	/	/	0	0	/	/
New Jersey									
Atlantic Co.	855	1	0	0	0	0	0	0	0
Bergen Co.[a,b]	792	1	0	/	/	2	0	/	/
Camden Co. Corr. Fac.[b]	1,237	2	1	0	0	0	0	/	/
Essex Co. Corr. Fac.	2,878	1	0	2	1	0	0	1	1
Monmouth Co. Corr. Inst.[a]	1,127	3	0	/	/	1	0	0	0
Ocean Co. Justice Complex	581	5	0	3	0	1	0	0	0
Passaic Co.	1,021	2	0	0	0	0	0	0	0
New Mexico									
Bernalillo Co. Metropolitan Det. Ctr.[a]	2,450	11	2	/	/	0	0	0	0
Guadalupe Co.[b]	62	1	0	0	0	0	0	/	/
New York									
Erie Co. Holding Ctr.[a,b]	1,311	2	1	/	/	0	0	/	/
Monroe Co.	1,433	0	0	1	1	0	0	0	0
New York City	12,421	15	0	9	0	83	3	4	0
Oneida Co.[a,b]	430	1	0	/	/	0	0	/	/
Suffolk Co.	1,784	0	0	0	0	3	0	1	0
Westchester Co.	1,468	4	0	4	0	2	0	0	0
North Carolina									
Durham Co. Det. Ctr.[a,b]	516	1	0	/	/	0	0	/	/
Pitt Co.	485	0	0	0	0	0	0	1	0
Wake Co.[a,b]	1,192	1	0	/	/	0	0	/	/
North Dakota									
Grand Forks Co. Corr. Ctr.	174	0	0	0	0	1	0	0	0
Ohio									
Butler Co.	889	0	0	0	0	1	0	0	0
Cuyahoga Co. Corr. Ctr.	2,114	4	0	12	0	5	0	0	0
Fairfield Co.	177	1	0	0	0	0	0	0	0
Franklin Co.[a]	1,916	4	0	/	/	0	0	0	0
Hamilton Co.	1,418	1	0	0	0	0	0	0	0
Lorain Co.	392	1	0	0	0	1	0	0	0

TABLE 4 (continued)
Allegations of sexual victimization reported by local jail authorities, by type of victimization, 2011

| | | Inmate-on-inmate | | | | Staff-on-inmate | | | |
| Jurisdiction and facility | Average daily population | Nonconsensual sexual acts | | Abusive sexual contact | | Sexual misconduct | | Sexual harassment | |
		Alleged	Substantiated	Alleged	Substantiated	Alleged	Substantiated	Alleged	Substantiated
Oklahoma									
Comanche Co. Det. Ctr.[a,b]	283	1	1	/	/	1	0	/	/
Grant Co.[c,e]	10	1	0	1	0	0	0	0	0
Le Flore Co. Det. Ctr.	171	1	0	0	0	0	0	0	0
Oklahoma Co.	2,115	12	1	2	1	0	0	0	0
Oregon									
Benton Co.[a]	66	1	0	/	/	2	0	0	0
Lane Co.	406	1	0	0	0	1	0	1	0
Marion Co.	507	0	0	0	0	3	0	0	0
Multnomah Co.	1,173	0	0	3	0	2	0	0	0
Pennsylvania									
Allegheny Co.	2,956	2	0	3	1	0	0	0	0
Berks Co. Prison	1,046	2	0	1	0	0	0	0	0
Bradford Co. Prison[a,b]	160	0	0	/	/	1	1	/	/
Chester Co. Prison[c,f]	940	0	0	/	/	1	0	0	0
Dauphin Co. Prison	943	1	0	1	0	3	0	0	0
Franklin Co.[d]	315	0	0	2	0	3	0	/	/
Lancaster Co. Prison	1,126	2	0	0	0	0	0	0	0
Lawrence Co. Corr.	245	1	0	0	0	0	0	0	/
Lehigh Co.	1,076	0	0	0	0	2	0	0	0
Lycoming Co. Prison	227	1	0	0	0	0	0	0	0
Mifflin Co.	82	0	0	0	0	1	1	2	1
Montgomery Co.	2,065	0	0	5	0	3	0	2	0
Northampton Co. Prison[a]	792	4	0	/	/	0	0	2	0
Philadelphia Prison Sys.[a]	7,951	1	0	/	/	5	0	9	9
Westmoreland Co. Prison[a,b]	524	1	0	/	/	0	0	/	/
York Co. Prison[g]	2,378	7	0	2	1	1	0	3	0
South Carolina									
Beaufort Co.	223	1	0	0	0	0	0	0	0
Charleston Co.[a]	1,553	0	0	/	/	6	2	0	0
Chesterfield Co.[a]	66	0	0	/	/	0	0	1	0
York Co.	394	0	0	0	0	1	0	0	0
Tennessee									
Blount Co.[a]	455	2	0	/	/	0	0	0	0
Davidson Co.	2,047	2	0	9	3	14	3	3	2
Hamilton Co.[a]	520	3	0	/	/	0	0	3	0
Perry Co.	45	0	0	0	0	1	0	0	0
Shelby Co.	2,677	21	0	2	0	1	1	1	0
Shelby Co. Govt. Div. of Corr.	2,393	2	1	0	0	0	0	0	0
Sumner Co.	657	0	0	0	0	1	0	0	0
Unicoi Co.	80	1	0	0	0	0	0	0	0
Texas									
Bexar Co.	3,854	6	0	4	0	8	1	0	0
Brazos Co.[a,b]	596	1	0	/	/	2	1	/	/
Coryell Co.[b]	85	0	0	0	0	1	0	/	/
Dallas Co.[a]	6,450	8	0	/	/	2	0	0	0
El Paso Co.	2,215	0	0	1	0	0	0	0	0
Galveston Co.	907	0	0	0	0	2	1	1	0
Harris Co.[a,b]	9,654	18	0	/	/	4	1	/	/
Hunt Co.	278	0	0	0	0	1	1	0	0
Jackson Co.	62	0	0	0	0	1	1	0	0
Johnson Co.	613	2	0	0	0	0	0	0	0
Tarrant Co.[c]	3,320	1	0	0	0	1	0	0	0
Travis Co.	2,414	1	1	5	4	4	1	4	0
Williamson Co.	627	0	0	0	0	2	0	0	0

TABLE 4 (continued)
Allegations of sexual victimization reported by local jail authorities, by type of victimization, 2011

		Inmate-on-inmate				Staff-on-inmate			
	Average daily	Nonconsensual sexual acts		Abusive sexual contact		Sexual misconduct		Sexual harassment	
Jurisdiction and facility	population	Alleged	Substantiated	Alleged	Substantiated	Alleged	Substantiated	Alleged	Substantiated
Utah									
Salt Lake Co.[a,b]	2,153	13	1	/	/	5	1	/	/
Utah Co.	820	1	1	3	2	0	0	0	0
Weber Co.[a]	799	6	0	/	/	0	0	3	0
Virginia									
Arlington Co.	434	1	1	0	0	0	0	0	0
Blue Ridge Reg. Jail	1,010	0	0	1	0	3	0	0	0
Chesapeake City	1,063	2	0	0	0	0	0	0	0
Fairfax Co. Adult Det. Ctr.	1,288	1	0	0	0	0	0	0	0
Hampton Roads Reg. Jail	1,198	1	0	1	0	1	0	0	0
Henrico Co.	1,283	4	0	3	1	0	0	0	0
Henry Co.	163	0	0	1	1	0	0	0	0
Norfolk City	1,336	0	0	3	0	0	0	0	0
Northwestern Reg. Adult Det. Ctr.	591	0	0	0	0	0	0	1	0
Pittsylvania Co.[a]	122	0	0	/	/	1	0	0	0
Richmond City	1,395	0	0	0	0	2	2	0	0
Riverside Reg. Jail	1,299	0	0	0	0	2	0	0	0
Southwest Virginia Reg. Jail	1,653	0	0	0	0	0	0	1	0
Virginia Beach City[a,b]	1,488	1	0	/	/	9	0	/	/
Western Tidewater Reg. Jail	669	1	0	1	0	2	0	0	0
Western Virginia Reg. Jail[b]	714	0	0	1	0	0	0	/	/
Washington									
Benton Co.	624	0	0	0	0	1	0	1	0
Columbia Co.	5	0	0	0	0	1	0	0	0
Cowlitz Co.	272	0	0	0	0	2	0	0	0
Grant Co.[a,b]	200	2	0	/	/	0	0	/	/
King Co.[a]	2,202	6	1	/	/	7	0	3	0
Kitsap Co. Corr. Ctr.	420	0	0	0	0	0	0	1	0
Pierce Co. Det. & Corr. Ctr.	1,244	5	0	2	0	2	0	1	0
Snohomish Co.	1,199	1	0	5	2	2	0	1	1
Spokane Co. (Geiger Corr. Ctr.)	764	0	0	19	2	5	0	0	0
Yakima Co.	700	1	0	0	0	0	0	0	0
West Virginia									
Central Reg. Jail	321	1	0	1	0	6	0	2	1
North Central Reg. Jail[a,b]	607	5	0	3	0	0	0	/	/
South Central Reg. Jail[d,f]	459	3	0	1	0	1	0	/	/
Tygart Valley Reg. Jail	413	1	0	0	0	2	1	0	0
Wisconsin									
Adams Co.	64	0	0	1	0	1	0	0	0
Kenosha Co.	833	1	0	7	1	1	0	0	0
Marathon Co. Adult Det. Fac.[a,b]	290	0	0	/	/	1	1	/	/
Milwaukee Co.	2,512	2	0	3	0	4	0	0	0
Outagamie Co.[a,b]	379	0	0	/	/	1	1	/	/
Racine Co.	687	0	0	1	0	1	1	0	0
Vilas Co.	87	0	0	1	1	0	0	0	0

/ Not reported.

[a]Allegations of abusive sexual contact could not be counted separately from allegations of nonconsensual sexual acts.

[b]Allegations of staff sexual harassment could not be counted separately from allegations of staff sexual misconduct.

[c]Counts of nonconsensual sexual acts were based on substantiated allegations only.

[d]Agency did not record allegations of staff sexual harassment.

[e]Counts of staff sexual misconduct were based on substantiated allegations only.

[f]Agency did not record allegations of abusive sexual contact.

[g]Average daily population was unavailable; the Deaths in Custody Reporting Program population was used in its place.

Source: Bureau of Justice Statistics, Survey of Sexual Violence, 2011.

TABLE 5
Allegations of sexual victimization reported by local jail authorities, by type of victimization, 2010

| | | Inmate-on-inmate | | | | Staff-on-inmate | | | |
| | Average daily | Nonconsensual sexual acts | | Abusive sexual contact | | Sexual misconduct | | Sexual harassment | |
Jurisdiction and facility	population	Alleged	Substantiated	Alleged	Substantiated	Alleged	Substantiated	Alleged	Substantiated
Total	307,608	455	59	188	41	290	39	90	10
Alabama									
Elmore Co.	252	0	0	0	0	5	0	5	0
Escambia Co.[a,b]	173	1	0	/	/	1	0	/	/
Macon Co.	9	0	0	0	0	2	0	0	0
Madison Co.[a]	1,019	3	0	/	/	1	0	0	0
Arizona									
Maricopa Co.[a,b]	7,555	19	6	/	/	4	0	/	/
Pima Co.	1,636	1	1	0	0	0	0	0	0
Yuma Co.	579	0	0	0	0	0	0	7	0
Arkansas									
Conway Co.[a,b]	43	0	0	/	/	2	0	/	/
Polk Co.[a]	24	0	0	/	/	1	0	0	0
Pope Co. Det. Ctr.	187	0	0	0	0	0	0	2	0
St. Francis Co.	93	1	0	1	0	0	0	0	0
California									
Alameda Co.[a,c]	3,821	1	1	/	/	0	0	0	0
Fresno Co.	1,874	2	0	1	0	0	0	0	0
Kern Co.	2,319	2	2	1	1	2	0	2	0
Los Angeles Co.[a]	16,624	16	0	/	/	1	0	1	0
Monterey Co.	1,048	1	0	0	0	0	0	0	0
Orange Co.[a]	5,051	3	1	/	/	1	0	0	0
Riverside Co.	3,253	4	1	0	0	0	0	0	0
San Bernardino Co. West Valley Det. Ctr.	5,803	3	3	1	1	0	0	0	0
San Diego Co.	4,646	6	1	0	0	2	0	0	0
San Francisco Co. & City[a]	1,788	5	0	/	/	6	1	0	0
San Joaquin Co.[c]	1,492	1	0	1	0	0	0	0	0
Santa Barbara Co.	978	0	0	0	0	1	1	0	0
Santa Clara Co.	3,837	1	0	1	0	1	0	1	0
Shasta Co.	227	1	0	0	0	0	0	0	0
Sonoma Co. Main Adult Det. Fac.	941	1	0	0	0	1	0	0	0
Stanislaus Co.[a,d,e]	1,257	1	0	/	/	/	/	/	/
Ventura Co.	1,586	2	1	1	0	0	0	0	0
Colorado									
Adams Co. Det. Fac.	1,289	0	0	1	1	0	0	0	0
Arapahoe Co.	1,221	1	0	2	0	0	0	0	0
Denver Co.	2,098	0	0	1	1	0	0	0	0
El Paso Co.	1,408	3	0	12	0	1	1	0	0
Jefferson Co.[a,b]	1,103	3	0	/	/	0	0	/	/
Larimer Co. Det. Ctr.[a,b]	489	1	0	/	/	0	0	/	/
Montezuma Co.	106	1	0	0	0	0	0	0	0
District of Columbia									
District of Columbia[a,b]	2,093	3	0	/	/	6	0	/	/
Florida									
Alachua Co.[a,f]	1,074	3	0	/	/	0	0	0	0
Brevard Co.[b]	1,585	2	0	1	0	0	0	/	/
Broward Co. Det. Ctr.	4,498	2	0	2	0	7	0	1	0
Hillsborough Co.[a]	3,277	3	0	/	/	0	0	0	0
Indian River Co.	518	0	0	1	0	0	0	0	0
Jacksonville City	3,932	7	2	3	2	0	0	0	0
Lake Co. Det. Ctr.[a,b]	1,009	1	0	/	/	0	0	/	/
Manatee Co.	1,074	7	0	2	0	1	0	1	0
Marion Co.	1,648	1	1	1	1	0	0	0	0
Miami-Dade Co. Corr. & Rehab	5,961	5	0	0	0	15	1	0	0

TABLE 5 (continued)
Allegations of sexual victimization reported by local jail authorities, by type of victimization, 2010

| | | Inmate-on-inmate | | | | Staff-on-inmate | | | |
| | | Nonconsensual sexual acts | | Abusive sexual contact | | Sexual misconduct | | Sexual harassment | |
Jurisdiction and facility	Average daily population	Alleged	Substantiated	Alleged	Substantiated	Alleged	Substantiated	Alleged	Substantiated
Orange Co.	3,572	2	0	1	0	1	0	0	0
Osceola Co.	993	0	0	0	0	2	0	0	0
Palm Beach Co.[a]	2,818	10	0	/	/	1	0	1	0
Pasco Co.[b]	1,354	2	1	1	0	0	0	/	/
Polk Co.	2,194	6	0	0	0	3	0	0	0
St. Lucie Co.	1,256	7	0	0	0	0	0	0	0
Sumter Co.[a,b]	220	1	0	/	/	0	0	/	/
Volusia Co. Division of Corr.	1,369	0	0	0	0	1	0	1	0
Georgia									
Berrien Co.	80	0	0	0	0	1	0	0	0
Chatham Co.[a]	2,044	5	3	/	/	1	0	0	0
Clayton Co.[b]	1,580	1	0	0	0	/	/	/	/
Cobb Co. Jail & Prison	2,200	2	0	1	0	0	0	0	0
Decatur Co. Prison[a,b]	349	2	0	/	/	0	0	/	/
Dekalb Co.[a,b]	3,383	1	0	/	/	0	0	/	/
Fulton Co.[a]	2,882	12	0	/	/	0	0	0	0
Gwinnett Co. Det. Ctr.	2,655	0	0	1	1	2	0	0	0
Tift Co.	214	1	0	0	0	3	0	2	0
Troup Co. Jail	430	0	0	0	0	1	1	0	0
Walker Co.	221	1	0	0	0	0	0	0	0
Idaho									
Ada Co.	971	1	0	0	0	0	0	0	0
Bannock Co.	255	4	0	0	0	1	0	0	0
Kootenai Co.[a]	300	1	1	/	/	0	0	0	0
Nez Perce Det. Fac.	97	1	0	0	0	0	0	0	0
Illinois									
Cook Co.	9,004	16	1	0	0	2	1	1	0
Kane Co.	654	0	0	0	0	0	0	2	0
Indiana									
Crawford Co.	58	2	0	0	0	0	0	0	0
Jefferson Co.[g]	81	0	0	0	0	0	0	2	0
Noble Co.[a,b]	176	0	0	/	/	1	0	/	/
Vanderburgh Co.[a,b]	623	0	0	/	/	1	1	/	/
Kansas									
Sedgwick Co. Det. Ctr.	1,576	2	1	0	0	5	2	0	0
Shawnee Co.	495	3	0	5	3	3	1	2	2
Kentucky									
Fayette Co. Det. Ctr.	1,251	0	0	2	2	3	1	2	0
Louisville Metropolitan[a,b]	1,930	2	0	/	/	2	1	/	/
Pulaski Co. Det. Ctr.[g]	276	2	0	0	0	0	0	0	0
Louisiana									
Bossier Parish	1,223	0	0	1	1	0	0	0	0
Caddo Parish Corr. Ctr.	1,365	0	0	0	0	0	0	1	1
Calvasieu Parish Corr. Ctr.	1,238	3	0	0	0	0	0	0	0
La Salle Management	243	0	0	0	0	1	0	0	0
Orleans Parish Prison	3,427	1	0	2	0	0	0	0	0
Rapides Parish[c]	1,024	0	0	4	0	0	0	0	0
St. Mary Parish	374	0	0	0	0	1	0	2	0
St. Tammany Parish	1,113	1	0	2	0	1	1	0	0
Maryland									
Anne Arundel Co.	878	11	1	0	0	0	0	0	0
Baltimore City Det. Ctr.[a,b]	3,582	4	0	/	/	1	0	/	/
Baltimore Co.	1,293	4	0	3	0	2	0	0	0
Charles Co. Det. Ctr.	433	0	0	4	4	0	0	0	0
Howard Co.[a,b]	293	2	0	/	/	0	0	/	/
Montgomery Co. Det. Ctr.	900	1	0	2	0	5	0	2	0

TABLE 5 (continued)
Allegations of sexual victimization reported by local jail authorities, by type of victimization, 2010

| | | Inmate-on-inmate | | | | Staff-on-inmate | | | |
| | Average daily population | Nonconsensual sexual acts | | Abusive sexual contact | | Sexual misconduct | | Sexual harassment | |
Jurisdiction and facility		Alleged	Substantiated	Alleged	Substantiated	Alleged	Substantiated	Alleged	Substantiated
Massachusetts									
Barnstable Co.	424	0	0	1	0	0	0	0	0
Bristol Co.	1,403	11	4	8	4	2	1	0	0
Hampden Co.	1,614	1	0	2	0	6	0	0	0
Middlesex Co. Billerica House of Corr.	807	0	0	1	0	0	0	0	0
Plymouth Co. House of Corr.[a]	1,412	1	0	/	/	0	0	0	0
Suffolk Co. House of Corr.	1,456	12	1	5	0	3	1	2	1
Michigan									
Berrien Co.	361	0	0	3	0	0	0	0	0
Lapeer Co.	119	0	0	1	0	0	0	0	0
Livingston Co.[f,g]	254	1	0	0	0	0	0	0	0
Macomb Co.[a]	1,165	1	0	/	/	0	0	0	0
Oakland Co.	1,517	3	2	0	0	1	1	0	0
Wayne Co.	1,950	8	1	0	0	0	0	0	0
Minnesota									
Hennepin Co. Adult Det. Ctr.[a,b]	685	1	0	/	/	0	0	/	/
Ramsey Co. Corr. Fac.[a]	446	1	1	/	/	0	0	1	0
Mississippi									
Bolivar Co. Corr. Fac.[a]	7	0	0	/	/	0	0	1	0
Harrison Co.	942	1	0	1	0	2	1	0	0
Lincoln Co.	87	0	0	0	0	1	1	0	0
Rankin Co.	411	0	0	0	0	1	1	0	0
Missouri									
Cass Co.[a]	103	1	0	/	/	0	0	0	0
Jackson Co. Det. Ctr.	866	0	0	1	0	1	0	1	0
McDonald Co.	36	0	0	0	0	1	0	0	0
Pulaski Co.[a,f,g,h]	61	0	0	/	/	1	1	0	0
St. Louis Co.	1,135	1	0	0	0	2	0	0	0
Montana									
Yellowstone Co. Det. Fac.[a,b,g]	379	1	0	/	/	0	0	/	/
Nebraska									
Douglas Co.	1,160	1	0	2	0	2	0	4	0
Lincoln Co.	70	1	0	1	0	0	0	0	0
Nevada									
Clark Co. Det. Ctr.	3,211	2	0	4	0	8	0	3	0
Washoe Co. Det. Ctr.	1,151	2	0	3	0	0	0	0	0
New Hampshire									
Strafford Co.[a,b]	455	2	0	/	/	2	0	/	/
Sullivan Co.	74	4	0	1	0	0	0	0	0
New Jersey									
Atlantic Co.	866	2	0	2	0	0	0	0	0
Camden Co. Corr. Fac.[b]	1,341	3	1	2	1	1	0	/	/
Hudson Co. Corr. Fac.	2,000	6	1	0	0	3	3	8	2
Middlesex Co. Adult Corr. Ctr.[a,b]	976	1	0	/	/	0	0	/	/
Monmouth Co. Corr. Inst.[a]	1,054	1	0	/	/	0	0	0	0
Somerset Co.	254	1	0	0	0	0	0	0	0
Union Co.	1,418	2	0	0	0	0	0	0	0
New Mexico									
Bernalillo Co. Metropolitan Det. Ctr.	2,450	2	0	2	0	1	0	0	0
Dona Ana Co. Det. Ctr.[a,b]	792	2	0	/	/	0	0	/	/
New York									
Franklin Co.	798	1	1	0	0	1	0	0	0
Monroe Co.	1,479	1	0	0	0	1	0	0	0

TABLE 5 (continued)
Allegations of sexual victimization reported by local jail authorities, by type of victimization, 2010

Jurisdiction and facility	Average daily population	Inmate-on-inmate				Staff-on-inmate			
		Nonconsensual sexual acts		Abusive sexual contact		Sexual misconduct		Sexual harassment	
		Alleged	Substantiated	Alleged	Substantiated	Alleged	Substantiated	Alleged	Substantiated
Nassau Co. Corr. Ctr.[h]	1,497	1	1	0	0	2	0	0	0
New York City	13,023	9	0	10	1	27	2	8	0
Westchester Co.	1,406	2	1	1	1	1	0	0	0
North Carolina									
Craven Co.[a,f]	293	2	1	/	/	0	0	0	0
Mecklenburg Co.	2,233	3	0	0	0	1	0	0	0
North Dakota									
Grand Forks Co. Corr. Ctr.[a,b]	176	0	0	/	/	1	0	/	/
Pierce Co.	130	2	0	0	0	0	0	0	0
Ohio									
Corr. Ctr. of Northwest Ohio	532	0	0	7	1	12	0	2	0
Cuyahoga Co. Corr. Ctr.	2,095	5	1	9	0	7	0	1	0
Franklin Co.[a,b]	1,915	3	0	/	/	0	0	/	/
Hamilton Co.	1,437	3	0	5	1	0	0	0	0
Licking Co.	241	0	0	1	0	0	0	0	0
Lorain Co.	391	1	0	2	0	0	0	0	0
Southeastern Ohio Reg. Jail	192	0	0	1	0	0	0	0	0
Tuscarawas Co.[b]	94	0	0	0	0	1	0	/	/
Oklahoma									
McIntosh Co.	171	0	0	0	0	1	0	0	0
Oklahoma Co.[a,b]	2,281	7	1	/	/	1	0	/	/
Osage Co.	112	0	0	0	0	2	0	0	0
Oregon									
Benton Co.	73	0	0	0	0	1	0	0	0
Marion Co.	515	0	0	2	2	6	0	0	0
Multnomah Co.	1,242	3	0	3	0	9	1	1	0
Yamhill Co.	219	0	0	0	0	1	0	0	0
Pennsylvania									
Berks Co. Prison	1,048	1	1	0	0	1	0	0	0
Bucks Co.	1,088	0	0	2	1	0	0	0	0
Dauphin Co. Prison	943	1	0	1	0	0	0	0	0
Lebanon Co. Prison[a,b]	453	1	1	/	/	0	0	/	/
Lehigh Co.	1,353	1	0	0	0	0	0	0	0
Mercer Co. Prison	257	0	0	1	0	1	0	0	0
Monroe Co.[a]	383	0	0	/	/	2	0	0	0
Montgomery Co.	1,753	2	0	0	0	0	0	0	0
Northampton Co. Prison	795	1	0	1	0	0	0	1	0
Schuylkill Co. Prison[a,b]	273	0	0	/	/	1	1	/	/
York Co. Prison[a,b,c]	2,299	3	0	/	/	0	0	/	/
South Carolina									
Charleston Co.[a]	1,738	1	0	/	/	0	0	5	1
Greenville Co.[a,b]	1,174	3	1	/	/	0	0	/	/
Kershaw Co.	80	1	0	1	0	0	0	0	0
Tennessee									
Carter Co.	194	0	0	0	0	1	1	0	0
Davidson Co.	2,429	9	1	3	2	9	1	2	1
Giles Co.	125	0	0	0	0	2	1	0	0
Hardin Co.	122	0	0	0	0	1	1	0	0
Hickman Co.	104	0	0	0	0	2	0	0	0
Knox Co.	1,068	1	0	2	1	0	0	0	0
Maury Co.[a,b]	266	0	0	/	/	1	0	/	/
McMinn Co.	225	1	0	0	0	1	0	0	0
Montgomery Co.[b]	365	1	0	0	0	0	0	/	/
Rutherford Co.[a]	688	1	0	/	/	0	0	0	0
Shelby Co.	2,699	13	0	0	0	0	0	0	0

TABLE 5 (continued)
Allegations of sexual victimization reported by local jail authorities, by type of victimization, 2010

Jurisdiction and facility	Average daily population	Inmate-on-inmate				Staff-on-inmate			
		Nonconsensual sexual acts		Abusive sexual contact		Sexual misconduct		Sexual harassment	
		Alleged	Substantiated	Alleged	Substantiated	Alleged	Substantiated	Alleged	Substantiated
Texas									
Aransas Co.	185	0	0	0	0	1	0	0	0
Bexar Co.	4,213	1	0	1	0	0	0	1	1
Cooke Co.	118	0	0	0	0	1	0	0	0
Dallas Co.[a]	6,790	5	3	/	/	0	0	0	0
Gregg Co.	770	1	0	0	0	0	0	0	0
Guadalupe Co.	411	0	0	0	0	1	0	0	0
Harris Co.[a,b]	9,026	17	3	/	/	2	2	/	/
Hunt Co.	263	2	0	0	0	2	2	0	0
Nueces Co.[a]	916	0	0	/	/	0	0	1	0
Terry Co.	104	0	0	0	0	1	1	0	0
Travis Co.	2,696	0	0	0	0	1	0	0	0
Utah									
Davis Co.	651	0	0	8	2	0	0	0	0
Salt Lake Co.[b]	2,149	2	0	5	0	0	0	/	/
Sevier Co.[a]	104	1	0	/	/	0	0	0	0
Virginia									
Fairfax Co. Adult Det. Ctr.	1,229	0	0	1	0	2	0	0	0
Hampton City[a]	369	0	0	/	/	1	0	0	0
Hampton Roads Reg. Jail	1,248	8	1	0	0	4	1	2	0
Henrico Co.	1,167	3	0	2	1	0	0	0	0
Norfolk City	1,325	3	0	3	0	0	0	0	0
Northwestern Reg. Adult Det. Ctr.[a]	571	0	0	/	/	3	0	0	0
Riverside Reg. Jail	1,208	1	0	0	0	3	0	1	0
Roanoke City	586	1	0	0	0	0	0	0	0
Southwest Virginia Reg. Jail	1,516	1	0	0	0	0	0	0	0
Virginia Beach City	1,374	1	0	0	0	2	0	0	0
Washington									
Chelan Co. Reg. Justice Ctr.[a,f,g]	282	1	0	/	/	0	0	0	0
Clark Co.	685	0	0	8	3	5	0	1	0
King Co.[a]	2,274	3	0	/	/	10	2	3	0
Pierce Co. Det. & Corr. Ctr.[a,b]	1,301	3	0	/	/	0	0	/	/
Snohomish Co.	1,163	0	0	4	1	4	0	1	0
Spokane Co. (Geiger Corr. Ctr.)[a]	546	0	0	/	/	1	0	0	0
Yakima Co.[a]	1,075	1	1	/	/	0	0	0	0
West Virginia									
Eastern Reg. Jail[a]	389	1	0	/	/	0	0	0	0
Southern Reg. Jail	467	0	0	0	0	0	0	1	1
Wisconsin									
Milwaukee Co.	2,629	1	0	2	1	3	0	0	0
Shawano Co.[a]	179	4	1	/	/	0	0	0	0
Waukesha Co.	628	1	0	0	0	0	0	0	0
Wyoming									
Laramie Co.[a]	177	1	1	/	/	2	0	1	0

/ Not reported.

[a]Allegations of abusive sexual contact could not be counted separately from allegations of nonconsensual sexual acts.

[b]Allegations of staff sexual harassment could not be counted separately from allegations of staff sexual misconduct.

[c]Average daily population was unavailable; the Deaths in Custody Reporting Program population was used in its place.

[d]Agency did not record allegations of staff sexual misconduct.

[e]Agency did not record allegations of staff sexual harassment.

[f]Counts of staff sexual misconduct were based on substantiated allegations only.

[g]Counts of nonconsensual sexual acts were based on substantiated allegations only.

[h]Counts of nonconsensual sexual acts were based on completed acts only.

Source: Bureau of Justice Statistics, Survey of Sexual Violence, 2010.

TABLE 6
Allegations of sexual victimization reported by local jail authorities, by type of victimization, 2009

Jurisdiction and facility	Average daily population	Inmate-on-inmate				Staff-on-inmate			
		Nonconsensual sexual acts		Abusive sexual contact		Sexual misconduct		Sexual harassment	
		Alleged	Substantiated	Alleged	Substantiated	Alleged	Substantiated	Alleged	Substantiated
Total	335,112	414	49	164	32	294	67	60	9
Alabama									
Houston Co.[a,b]	480	1	1	/	/	0	0	/	/
Mobile Co.	1,252	1	0	0	0	0	0	0	0
Alaska									
Kotzebue Reg. Jail	15	0	0	0	0	1	0	0	0
Arizona									
Gila Co.[a,b]	153	1	0	/	/	0	0	/	/
Maricopa Co.	8,624	6	0	7	1	11	0	10	0
Pima Co.	1,826	1	0	0	0	0	0	0	0
Yavapi Co.	492	0	0	1	1	0	0	0	0
Arkansas									
Craighead Co. Det. Ctr.	348	0	0	1	0	0	0	0	0
California									
Alameda Co.[a,b]	4,395	1	1	/	/	1	1	/	/
Contra Costa Co.[b]	1,695	2	1	1	1	1	0	/	/
El Dorado Co.	358	0	0	0	0	1	0	0	0
Fresno Co.	2,736	8	0	0	0	3	0	0	0
Kern Co.	2,277	0	0	0	0	2	2	1	0
Los Angeles Co.[a]	19,080	14	2	/	/	1	1	1	1
Orange Co.[b]	5,550	0	0	0	0	4	2	/	/
Rio Consumnes Corr. Ctr.	2,195	1	0	1	0	0	0	0	0
Riverside Co.	3,558	6	1	0	0	1	1	0	0
Sacramento Co.	4,302	1	0	1	1	0	0	0	0
San Bernardino Co. West Valley Det. Ctr.	6,080	0	0	0	0	2	1	0	0
San Diego Co.	4,991	2	0	0	0	2	0	0	0
San Francisco Co. & City	1,971	1	0	5	0	3	0	1	0
San Joaquin Co.	1,467	1	0	1	0	1	0	0	0
San Luis Obispo Co.	563	1	0	0	0	0	0	0	0
Santa Barbara Co.	1,267	1	0	1	0	0	0	0	0
Santa Clara Co.[a]	3,874	3	2	/	/	2	1	3	2
Solano Co.	947	1	0	1	0	0	0	0	0
Sonoma Co. Main Adult Det. Fac.[b]	1,022	0	0	1	1	0	0	/	/
Ventura Co.	807	0	0	1	1	0	0	0	0
Colorado									
Denver Co.	1,926	1	0	0	0	0	0	0	0
Douglas Co.[a,b]	323	1	1	/	/	0	0	/	/
Jefferson Co.[b]	1,386	3	0	3	32	3	0	/	/
La Plata Co.	124	1	0	0	0	0	0	0	0
Larimer Co. Det. Ctr.	469	0	0	1	0	0	0	0	0
District of Columbia									
District of Columbia	1,907	5	0	5	0	0	0	0	0
Florida									
Brevard Co.	1,481	2	0	1	0	1	0	0	0
Broward Co. Det. Ctr.	4,888	1	0	1	0	11	0	0	0
DeSoto Co.[a,b]	184	1	0	/	/	0	0	/	/
Escambia Co.	1,562	1	0	1	0	1	0	0	0
Jacksonville City	3,830	4	3	3	1	0	0	0	0
Lake Co. Det. Ctr.[c]	1,035	1	0	0	0	0	0	0	0
Lee Co.[c]	1,900	0	0	0	0	2	0	0	0
Manatee Co.	1,165	1	0	0	0	1	0	0	0
Miami-Dade Co. Corr. & Rehab	6,051	4	0	0	0	19	5	1	0
Okeechobee Co.[a]	244	0	0	/	/	1	1	0	0
Orange Co.	3,836	1	0	4	2	3	0	0	0

TABLE 6 (continued)
Allegations of sexual victimization reported by local jail authorities, by type of victimization, 2009

Jurisdiction and facility	Average daily population	Inmate-on-inmate				Staff-on-inmate			
		Nonconsensual sexual acts		Abusive sexual contact		Sexual misconduct		Sexual harassment	
		Alleged	Substantiated	Alleged	Substantiated	Alleged	Substantiated	Alleged	Substantiated
Florida (continued)									
Osceola Co.[a]	1,047	1	0	/	/	0	0	0	0
Palm Beach Co.	2,755	3	0	0	0	5	2	0	0
Pasco Co.	1,301	1	0	2	0	2	0	0	0
Pinellas Co.[a,b]	3,192	3	0	/	/	0	0	/	/
Polk Co.	2,327	9	1	2	1	1	1	1	0
Sarasota Co.	871	0	0	0	0	2	0	1	1
Seminole Co. John E. Polk Corr. Fac.	961	3	0	0	0	0	0	0	0
St. Lucie Co.	1,383	9	0	0	0	0	0	0	0
Volusia Co. Division of Corr.	1,385	3	0	2	1	0	0	0	0
Georgia									
Atlanta City Det. Ctr.	838	1	1	0	0	4	0	2	0
Chatham Co.	1,718	5	3	1	1	0	0	0	0
Clayton Co.[a]	1,897	0	0	/	/	1	0	0	0
Columbia Co. Det. Ctr.[a]	239	1	1	/	/	0	0	0	0
Dekalb Co.[a,b]	3,360	4	1	/	/	1	1	/	/
Gwinnett Co. Det. Ctr.	2,671	2	0	0	0	3	0	0	0
Muscogee Co.[a,b]	1,171	1	0	/	/	1	0	/	/
Wayne Co.	129	1	0	1	0	0	0	0	0
Idaho									
Ada Co.	987	2	1	1	0	0	0	0	0
Twin Falls Adult Criminal Justice Fac.	213	0	0	0	0	0	0	1	1
Illinois									
Cook Co.	9,039	9	1	3	0	0	0	0	0
Jackson Co.[a,b]	118	1	0	/	/	0	0	/	/
Lake Co.[a,b]	603	1	0	/	/	0	0	/	/
Lawrence Co.	33	0	0	0	0	1	1	0	0
Winnebago Co.[a]	801	3	0	/	/	0	0	0	0
Indiana									
Clark Co.	406	0	0	1	0	2	1	0	0
Clinton Co.	181	1	1	0	0	0	0	0	0
Hendricks Co.	244	0	0	0	0	2	0	0	0
Marion Co.	1,281	0	0	3	0	0	0	0	0
Montgomery Co.	204	1	0	0	0	0	0	0	0
Scott Co. Security Ctr.	100	2	0	0	0	0	0	0	0
Kansas									
Butler Co.[d]	200	0	0	0	0	0	0	1	0
Johnson Co. Adult Det. Ctr.	751	0	0	0	0	1	1	0	0
Sedgwick Co. Det. Ctr.	1,645	5	0	5	0	5	1	0	0
Kentucky									
Bullitt Co.	312	6	0	2	0	2	0	0	0
Fayette Co. Det. Ctr.	1,201	0	0	0	0	4	0	1	0
Fulton Co. Det. Ctr.[a,e]	251	1	0	/	/	0	0	0	0
Lincoln Co. Reg. Jail	97	0	0	0	0	1	0	0	0
Louisville Metropolitan	1,909	4	0	0	0	5	0	0	0
Ohio Co. Det. Ctr.[a]	62	2	2	/	/	0	0	0	0
Shelby Co. Det. Ctr.	305	2	0	0	0	1	0	2	0
Louisiana									
Bossier Parish	1,170	1	1	0	0	0	0	0	0
Caddo Parish Corr. Ctr.	1,242	0	0	0	0	0	0	1	0
Calvasieu Parish Corr. Ctr.	1,223	3	0	0	0	0	0	1	0
East Baton Rouge Parish Prison[e]	1,682	3	0	0	0	1	1	0	0
Lafayette Parish	931	1	0	0	0	4	3	0	0
Orleans Parish Prison	3,239	6	2	1	0	0	0	0	0
Rapides Parish	941	0	0	1	0	0	0	0	0

TABLE 6 (continued)
Allegations of sexual victimization reported by local jail authorities, by type of victimization, 2009

Jurisdiction and facility	Average daily population	Inmate-on-inmate				Staff-on-inmate			
		Nonconsensual sexual acts		Abusive sexual contact		Sexual misconduct		Sexual harassment	
		Alleged	Substantiated	Alleged	Substantiated	Alleged	Substantiated	Alleged	Substantiated
Maine									
Cumberland Co.	428	2	1	0	0	0	0	0	0
Somerset Co.[a,b,c]	131	2	0	/	/	2	0	/	/
Maryland									
Anne Arundel Co.	1,106	3	0	0	0	1	0	0	0
Baltimore City Det. Ctr.[a,b]	3,871	5	0	/	/	2	1	/	/
Baltimore Co.	1,332	3	0	0	0	0	0	0	0
Carroll Co. Det. Ctr.[a]	268	1	0	/	/	0	0	0	0
Montgomery Co. Det. Ctr.	850	1	0	2	0	0	0	0	0
Prince George's Co. Corr. Ctr.	1,259	1	0	0	0	1	1	0	0
Massachusetts									
Berkshire Co.	343	0	0	1	0	1	1	0	0
Bristol Co.	1,355	7	2	17	7	3	0	0	0
Hampden Co.	1,752	2	0	0	0	1	1	0	0
Suffolk Co.	716	0	0	1	0	0	0	0	0
Suffolk Co. House of Corr.	1,684	9	1	12	2	3	0	0	0
Worcester Co. Jail & House of Corr.[a,b]	1,200	4	1	/	/	0	0	/	/
Michigan									
Macomb Co.	1,253	1	0	0	0	0	0	0	0
Oakland Co.	1,727	0	0	2	0	1	0	0	0
Ottawa Co.	352	1	0	0	0	0	0	0	0
Wayne Co.	2,112	1	0	1	1	1	1	0	0
Minnesota									
Dakota Co.[e,f]	235	1	0	0	0	0	0	/	/
Hennepin Co. Adult Corr. Fac.	549	0	0	0	0	2	0	0	0
Scott Co.[a,b]	133	1	0	/	/	0	0	/	/
Mississippi									
Desoto Co.	401	0	0	1	0	0	0	0	0
Harrison Co.	705	1	0	1	0	0	0	0	0
Lowndes Co.[a,b]	222	1	1	/	/	0	0	/	/
Madison Co.[a,b]	360	9	0	/	/	0	0	/	/
Missouri									
Jackson Co. Det. Ctr.	970	0	0	0	0	1	1	0	0
Jefferson Co.[b]	194	0	0	0	0	1	1	/	/
Scott Co.[a]	104	0	0	/	/	2	2	0	0
St. Louis Co.	1,167	0	0	2	1	2	0	2	0
Montana									
Cascade Co. Reg. Jail[a,b]	334	6	0	/	/	1	0	/	/
Nebraska									
Douglas Co.[a,b]	1,194	7	2	/	/	1	0	/	/
Nevada									
Clark Co. Det. Ctr.	3,108	2	0	4	4	0	0	0	0
Washoe Co. Det. Ctr.[a]	1,204	9	1	/	/	0	0	0	0
New Hampshire									
Hillsborough Co. House of Corr.	598	0	0	0	0	1	0	0	0
New Jersey									
Camden Co. Corr. Fac.[a,b]	1,686	3	0	/	/	1	0	/	/
Essex Co. Corr. Fac.[b]	2,467	2	0	0	0	0	0	/	/
Hudson Co. Corr. Fac.	1,834	2	0	2	0	0	0	0	0
Middlesex Co. Adult Corr. Ctr.[a,b,e,g]	1,224	1	0	/	/	0	0	/	/
Monmouth Co. Corr. Inst.	1,085	1	0	0	0	0	0	0	0
Ocean Co. Justice Complex	514	1	0	0	0	0	0	0	0
Passaic Co.	1,190	1	0	0	0	0	0	0	0
Somerset Co.	317	1	0	0	0	0	0	0	0

TABLE 6 (continued)
Allegations of sexual victimization reported by local jail authorities, by type of victimization, 2009

		Inmate-on-inmate				Staff-on-inmate			
		Nonconsensual sexual acts		Abusive sexual contact		Sexual misconduct		Sexual harassment	
Jurisdiction and facility	Average daily population	Alleged	Substantiated	Alleged	Substantiated	Alleged	Substantiated	Alleged	Substantiated
New Jersey (continued)									
Sussex Co. Keogh Dwyer Corr. Fac.	149	1	0	0	0	0	0	1	0
Union Co.	1,081	1	0	0	0	0	0	0	0
New Mexico									
Bernalillo Co. Metropolitan Det. Ctr.	2,519	10	3	5	0	2	2	0	0
Eddy Co. Det. Ctr.	238	0	0	0	0	1	1	0	0
New York									
Allegany Co.[a]	135	0	0	/	/	0	0	1	0
Erie Co. Holding Ctr.	1,345	0	0	4	0	5	0	1	0
Nassau Co. Corr. Ctr.[c]	1,579	0	0	0	0	3	0	0	0
New York City	13,198	6	0	1	0	33	0	5	0
Niagara Co.[a,b]	498	0	0	/	/	1	1	/	/
Rensselaer Co.	214	0	0	0	0	0	0	1	0
Suffolk Co.[a]	1,663	0	0	/	/	4	0	0	0
Westchester Co.[a,b]	1,407	0	0	/	/	1	0	/	/
North Carolina									
Cabarrus Co.	271	1	0	0	0	0	0	0	0
Dare Co. Det. Ctr.	76	0	0	0	0	1	0	0	0
Lee Co.	114	0	0	0	0	1	0	0	0
Rutherford Co.[b]	209	1	0	0	0	0	0	/	/
Ohio									
Cuyahoga Co. Corr. Ctr.	1,830	2	0	3	0	5	0	0	0
Franklin Co.[a,b]	1,946	2	0	/	/	0	0	/	/
Hamilton Co.	1,438	4	0	0	0	0	0	0	0
Lorain Co.	410	1	0	0	0	1	0	0	0
Seneca Co.[b]	193	0	0	0	0	1	0	/	/
Tri-Co. Reg. Jail[a]	164	1	0	/	/	0	0	0	0
Oklahoma									
Muskogee Co. & City[a,e,g]	295	1	0	/	/	0	0	0	0
Sequoyah Co.[a]	108	1	0	/	/	0	0	0	0
Oregon									
Clackamas Co.	434	2	0	0	0	2	1	0	0
Josephine Co.	174	2	0	1	0	0	0	0	0
Linn Co.	206	1	1	0	0	0	0	0	0
Multnomah Co.	1,316	0	0	2	1	4	0	1	0
Tillamook Co.	83	2	0	0	0	0	0	0	0
Pennsylvania									
Allegheny Co.	2,756	2	1	0	0	0	0	0	0
Berks Co. Prison	1,083	0	0	1	1	0	0	0	0
Bucks Co.	1,074	0	0	3	0	3	0	1	0
Columbia Co. Prison[a]	186	2	0	/	/	0	0	0	0
Cumberland Co. Prison[a]	367	0	0	/	/	0	0	1	0
Lancaster Co. Prison	1,154	1	0	0	0	1	1	0	0
Lehigh Co.	1,373	0	0	2	0	1	1	0	0
Monroe Co.[a]	359	0	0	/	/	0	0	1	0
Philadelphia Prison Sys.	8,716	12	2	0	0	8	6	0	0
York Co. Prison[h]	2,246	2	0	0	0	2	0	0	0
South Carolina									
Dorchester Co.[a,b]	229	2	0	/	/	0	0	/	/
Greenville Co.	1,303	0	0	0	0	2	2	0	0
Jasper Co.	145	1	1	0	0	0	0	0	0
Lexington Co.[a]	857	1	1	/	/	0	0	0	0

TABLE 6 (continued)
Allegations of sexual victimization reported by local jail authorities, by type of victimization, 2009

| | | Inmate-on-inmate | | | | Staff-on-inmate | | | |
| | | Nonconsensual sexual acts | | Abusive sexual contact | | Sexual misconduct | | Sexual harassment | |
Jurisdiction and facility	Average daily population	Alleged	Substantiated	Alleged	Substantiated	Alleged	Substantiated	Alleged	Substantiated
Tennessee									
Anderson Co.[a,b]	269	1	0	/	/	0	0	/	/
Carter Co.[a,b,e,g]	198	1	0	/	/	0	0	/	/
Davidson Co.	2,203	2	0	11	0	9	6	1	1
Giles Co.	137	0	0	0	0	1	0	0	0
Jackson Co.	100	0	0	0	0	1	1	0	0
McMinn Co.[a,c,e,g]	223	0	0	/	/	1	1	0	0
Montgomery Co.[a,b,c]	385	0	0	/	/	2	1	/	/
Roane Co.	150	1	0	0	0	1	0	0	0
Shelby Co.	2,751	1	0	2	0	0	0	0	0
Shelby Co. Govt. Div. of Corr.[a]	2,700	1	0	/	/	0	0	2	0
Texas									
Bexar Co.	4,439	0	0	0	0	8	0	0	0
Brazos Co.[b]	512	1	0	/	/	0	0	/	/
Crane Co.	14	0	0	0	0	1	0	1	0
Dallas Co.[a]	6,160	1	1	/	/	1	1	0	0
El Paso Co.[a,b]	2,057	2	0	/	/	0	0	/	/
Galveston Co.	937	1	0	0	0	0	0	1	0
Gregg Co.	729	0	0	0	0	2	0	0	0
Harris Co.[a]	11,013	21	0	/	/	3	1	0	0
Hidalgo Co.	1,064	1	1	2	2	0	0	0	0
Montgomery Co.[a,b]	884	2	0	/	/	0	0	/	/
Travis Co.	2,406	6	0	2	1	2	0	0	0
Utah									
Iron Co.[a]	131	0	0	/	/	2	2	0	0
Salt Lake Co.	2,078	3	1	3	0	0	0	0	0
Virginia									
Alexandria City	484	1	1	1	0	1	0	0	0
Blue Ridge Reg. Jail	1,269	1	0	0	0	0	0	0	0
Chesapeake City	1,085	0	0	0	0	1	0	0	0
Hampton Roads Reg. Jail	1,269	2	0	0	0	3	0	0	0
Henrico Co.[a,b]	1,249	2	0	/	/	0	0	/	/
Norfolk City	1,524	0	0	5	0	1	0	6	0
Northwestern Reg. Adult Det. Ctr.	397	3	0	0	0	0	0	0	0
Richmond City	1,463	0	0	0	0	1	0	1	0
Riverside Reg. Jail	1,146	0	0	0	0	2	0	0	0
Roanoke City	660	1	0	0	0	0	0	0	0
Southwest Virginia Reg. Jail	1,389	3	0	0	0	1	0	0	0
Washington									
King Co.[a]	2,403	5	0	/	/	3	0	1	0
Kitsap Co. Corr. Ctr.	372	0	0	1	0	2	1	0	0
Lewis Co.	202	1	0	0	0	1	0	0	0
Pierce Co. Det. & Corr. Ctr.[b]	1,261	1	0	0	0	3	0	/	/
Snohomish Co.	1,180	0	0	1	0	0	0	0	0
Yakima Co.	1,054	3	0	1	0	1	0	0	0
West Virginia									
Eastern Reg. Jail[a]	427	1	0	/	/	0	0	1	1
North Central Reg. Jail[a]	502	3	0	/	/	1	0	/	/
Western Reg. Jail[c,g]	541	1	0	0	0	0	0	0	0
Wisconsin									
Milwaukee Co.	918	4	0	1	0	2	2	0	0
Vilas Co.[a,b]	98	1	0	/	/	0	0	/	/
Walworth Co.	393	1	0	0	0	0	0	0	0

TABLE 6 (continued)
Allegations of sexual victimization reported by local jail authorities, by type of victimization, 2009

| | | Inmate-on-inmate | | | | Staff-on-inmate | | | |
| | Average daily population | Nonconsensual sexual acts | | Abusive sexual contact | | Sexual misconduct | | Sexual harassment | |
Jurisdiction and facility		Alleged	Substantiated	Alleged	Substantiated	Alleged	Substantiated	Alleged	Substantiated
Wyoming									
Campbell Co. Det. Ctr.[a]	162	0	0	/	/	0	0	1	0
Laramie Co.	197	0	0	0	0	0	0	2	2

/ Not reported.

[a]Allegations of abusive sexual contact could not be counted separately from allegations of nonconsensual sexual acts.

[b]Allegations of staff sexual harassment could not be counted separately from allegations of staff sexual misconduct.

[c]Counts of nonconsensual sexual acts were based on completed acts only.

[d]Agency did not record allegations of nonconsensual sexual acts.

[e]Counts of staff sexual misconduct were based on substantiated allegations only.

[f]Agency did not record allegations of staff sexual harassment.

[g]Counts of nonconsensual sexual acts were based on substantiated allegations only.

[h]Average daily population was unavailable; the Deaths in Custody Reporting Program population was used in its place.

Source: Bureau of Justice Statistics, Survey of Sexual Violence, 2009.

TABLE 7
Local jail authorities with no allegations of sexual victimization, 2011

Jurisdiction and facility	Average daily population	Jurisdiction and facility	Average daily population
Total	123,543	**Colorado**	
Alabama		Montrose Co.[b,d]	76
Albertville City	41	Otero Co.[a,b]	41
Alexander City	5	Park Co.	80
Carbon Hill City	3	Routt Co.[a,b]	25
Cherokee Co.	122	Sedgwick Co.[a]	2
Chilton Co.	195	Washington Co.[a,b]	160
Covington Co.[a,b]	200	**Florida**	
De Kalb Co.	258	Baker Co.	141
Hale Co.	43	Collier Co. Det. Ctr.	900
Irondale City	1	Escambia Co.	1,382
Jackson Co.	150	Gilchrist Co.	30
Marion Co.	104	Glades Co.	503
Montgomery City	332	Highlands Co.[a,b]	403
Montgomery Co.	526	Hillsborough Co.[a,b]	3,104
Orange Beach City	21	Jackson Co. Corr. Fac.	217
Tuscaloosa Co.	622	Lake Co. Det. Ctr.[b,d]	895
Walker Co.	218	Leon Co. Det. Fac.	966
Warrior City[c,d,e,f]	1	Monroe Co.[b]	576
Wilcox Co.[g]	50	Sumter Co.[b]	251
Alaska		Taylor Co.	75
Craig City	80	**Georgia**	
Kotzebue Reg. Jail	12	Athens-Clarke Co. Corr. Inst.[a,b]	108
Petersburg City[a,b]	1	Augusta-Richmond Co.	899
Arizona		Baldwin Co.	230
Navajo Co.[a,b]	299	Bank Co.	37
Arkansas		Bleckley Co.[h]	45
Benton Co.[b]	464	Burke Co.	133
Cabot City[a,b]	2	Carroll Co. Prison[a,b]	238
Carroll Co.	35	Cherokee Co.	548
Conway Co.[a,b]	51	Claxton City	2
Craighead Co. Det. Ctr.	326	Colquitt Co. Prison	180
Hempstead Co.	60	Coweta Co. Jail	350
Howard Co.[b]	30	Dade Co.	46
Jefferson Co.	260	Dawson Co.[a,b]	163
Lafayette Co.	22	Decatur Co.	124
Marion Co.[a,b]	12	Elbert Co.	60
Pulaski Co. Reg. Jail	1,310	Floyd Co. Prison	344
Saline Co. Det. Fac.[a]	148	Forsyth Co.	409
Sheridan City	70	Glynn Co. Det. Ctr.	459
California		Greene Co.[a]	74
Contra Costa Co.[a]	1,750	Gwinnett Co. Comprehensive Corr. Complex	434
El Dorado Co.	313	Hall Co. Det. Ctr.[a,b]	997
Glendale City	14	Irwin Co. Det. Ctr.[a,b]	751
Kings Co.[a]	480	Kennesaw City	15
Mariposa Co.	39	Mitchell Co.[a,b]	105
Merced Co.	925	Oconee Co.	68
Monterey Co.	1,015	Randolph Co.	23
Rio Consumnes Corr. Ctr.	1,898	Screven Co.	85
San Mateo Co.[a,b]	979	Sumter Co.	160
Solano Co.	944	Sumter Co. Prison[a]	343
Sutter Co.	205	Telfair Co.[b,g,i]	28
Ventura Co.	1,535	Whitfield Co.[a,b]	409
Yolo Co. Monroe Det. Ctr.	396	**Idaho**	
Yuba Co.	365	Ada Co.	949
		Idaho Co.	9
		Jerome Co.	61
		Owyhee Co.	23

TABLE 7 (continued)
Local jail authorities with no allegations of sexual victimization, 2011

Jurisdiction and facility	Average daily population	Jurisdiction and facility	Average daily population
Illinois		**Kentucky**	
Clay Co.	5	Boone Co.	454
Dewitt Co.	66	Calloway Co.[a,b,g,h]	157
Du Page Co.	813	Grant Co.Det. Ctr.[a]	323
Fayette Co.	33	Grayson Co. Det. Ctr.	589
Hancock Co.	20	Madison Co. Det. Ctr.[a,b]	271
Jersey Co.	32	McCracken Co. Reg. Jail	470
Knox Co.	138	McCreary Co.	77
Macon Co.[a]	290	Montgomery Co. Reg. Jail[a,b,g,h]	172
Madison Co.[a]	273	Muhlenberg Co. Det. Ctr.	247
Morgan Co.	52	Oldham Co.	115
Ogle Co.[a,b]	89	Russell Co. Det. Ctr.	97
Peoria Co.[a,b]	478	Wayne Co. Det. Ctr.	187
Indiana		**Louisiana**	
Boone Co.	131	Ascension Parish	494
Greene Co.[a]	68	Assumption Parish[a]	95
Hendricks Co.[b]	278	Avoyelles Parish	1,142
Howard Co.	307	Bossier Parish	1,212
Johnson Co.	285	East Baton Rouge Parish Prison[h]	1,605
Miami Co.	97	East Carroll Parish	748
Monroe Co.[a]	247	East Feliciana Parish Prison[b]	161
Morgan Co.[a,b]	290	Morehouse Parish	265
Porter Co.	418	Opelousas City[a,b]	42
Rush Co.	36	Ouachita Parish Corr. Ctr.	1,029
Shelby Co.	180	Rapides Parish	1,024
Warren Co.[a,b,i]	28	St. Charles Parish	535
Washington Co.[a,b]	76	St. Helena Parish	35
White Co.	114	St. John Parish	245
Iowa		Tangipahoa Parish	526
Adair Co.	3	Union Parish Det. Ctr.	383
Benton Co.	14	Vernon Parish Corr. Fac.[g,h,i]	223
Bremer Co.[a,b]	50	West Carroll Parish	24
Butler Co.	1	**Maryland**	
Cherokee Co.[g,h,i]	8	Prince George's Co. Corr. Ctr.	1,316
Hancock Co.	5	**Massachusetts**	
Hardin Co.[a]	79	Franklin Co.	222
Henry Co.	8	Plymouth Co. House of Corr.[a]	1,398
Lee Co.	44	Worcester Co. Jail & House of Corr.	1,450
Osceola Co.[a,b]	5	**Michigan**	
Page Co.	8	Barry Co.	82
Scott Co.[a]	234	Benzie Co.	31
Wapello Co.[a,b,h]	67	Genesee Co.[a,b]	542
Woodbury Co.	234	Gratiot Co.[a]	69
Kansas		Jackson Co.[a,b]	394
Bourbon Co.	48	Kalamazoo Co.	413
Cowley Co.	111	Lenawee Co.	222
Elk Co.	2	Macomb Co.[a,b]	1,128
Finney Co.[c,d,e,f]	126	Midland Co.[a]	220
Graham Co.	9	Montcalm Co.	148
Grant Co.[g]	24	Ontonagon Co.[a,b]	5
Johnson Co. Adult Det. Ctr.	685	Saginaw Co.	483
Lincoln Co.	4	**Minnesota**	
McPherson Co.	33	Arrowhead Reg. Corr.	128
Ness Co.	4	Brown Co.	23
Pawnee Co.	13	Douglas Co.[a]	68
		Hennepin Co. Adult Corr. Fac.	434
		Lyon Co.	47
		Morrison Co.	38

TABLE 7 (continued)
Local jail authorities with no allegations of sexual victimization, 2011

Jurisdiction and facility	Average daily population	Jurisdiction and facility	Average daily population
Minnesota (continued)		**New Jersey**	
Ramsey Co. Corr. Fac.	391	Hudson Co. Corr. Fac.	1,849
Redwood Co.	17	Middlesex Co. Adult Corr. Ctr.[g,h,i]	951
Watonwan Co.	9	Morris Co.	368
Mississippi		Salem Co.	267
Carroll-Montgomery Co. Reg. Corr. Ctr.	272	**New Mexico**	
Clay Co.	116	Dona Ana Co. Det. Ctr.[a,b]	831
Covington Co.[a]	30	Eddy Co. Det. Ctr.[a]	213
Desoto Co.	380	Los Alamos Co.[h]	18
George Co.	358	Sandoval Co.	327
Hollandale City	7	**New York**	
Humphreys Co.	32	Albany Co.[a]	622
Issaquena Co.	271	Chautauqua Co.[a]	271
Jackson Co.[a,b]	442	Columbia Co.	105
Jefferson-Franklin Co. Corr. Fac.	247	Lewis Co.	33
Kemper-Neshoba Co. Reg. Corr. Fac.	344	Nassau Co. Corr. Ctr.	1,497
Leake Co. Corr. Fac.[a]	340	Onondaga Co. Dept. of Corr. - Jamesville	488
Perry Co.	35	Onondaga Co. Justice Ctr.	640
Prentiss Co.[a,b]	68	Rockland Co.	245
Stone Co. Reg. Corr. Fac.	384	Steuben Co.	175
Tate Co.	81	Tompkins Co.	74
Yazoo Co.	452	Ulster Co.	331
Missouri		Wayne Co.	152
Barry Co.	66	**North Carolina**	
Dallas Co.	22	Buncombe Co.[a]	394
Ferguson City	13	Cabarrus Co.[a,b]	335
Harrison Co.	20	Chowan Co.	21
Hickory Co.	1	Forsyth Co.	653
Johnson Co.	71	Gaston Co.	512
Laclede Co.	105	Greene Co.	4
Perry Co.	25	Lee Co.[a,b]	105
Ray Co.[a,b,g,h]	120	Mecklenburg Co.	2,022
Schuyler Co.	3	Montgomery Co.[g,i]	70
St. Charles Co.	481	Moore Co.[a,g]	126
Sullivan Co.	1	Orange Co.[a]	144
Taney Co.[a,b,g,h]	128	Pamlico Co.	74
Wayne Co.[b]	17	Rowan Co.[a,b]	267
Montana		Sampson Co.[i]	200
Beaverhead Co.[a,b]	82	Vance Co.	151
Big Horn Co.	35	Yadkin Co.	47
Granite Co.	2	**North Dakota**	
Musselshell Co.	7	Bottineau Co.	4
Yellowstone Co. Det. Fac.	382	Richland Co.[a,b]	13
Nebraska		Stutsman Co.	69
Boone Co.	3	**Ohio**	
Custer Co.[a]	8	Clark Co.	193
Dawson Co.	117	Erie Co.	126
Knox Co.	4	Gallia Co.	55
Nemaha Co.[h]	10	Greene Co.	245
Pierce Co.[d]	16	Knox Co.	71
Saline Co.	68	Lake Co.[a,b]	314
Nevada		Lakewood City	8
Lander Co.	15	Lawrence Co.[b,g,i]	85
Las Vegas City	681	Mahoning Co.	365
Lyon Co.[a]	68	Niles City	3
New Hampshire		Summit Co. & Glenwood Annex	688
Belknap Co.[a]	115	Tri-Co. Reg. Jail[a,b]	158
Hillsborough Co. House of Corr.	534	Zanesville City[a]	40

TABLE 7 (continued)
Local jail authorities with no allegations of sexual victimization, 2011

Jurisdiction and facility	Average daily population	Jurisdiction and facility	Average daily population
Oklahoma		**Texas**	
Ada City	4	Archer Co.[a,b]	17
Alfalfa Co.	6	Bandera Co.	70
Bristow City[d]	3	Bastrop Co.	334
Cherokee Co.[a,b]	123	Brazoria Co.	870
Cotton Co.	41	Burnet Co.	146
Grady Co.	520	Cameron Co.[a,b]	1,423
Kay Co. Det. Ctr.[a]	170	Collin Co.	837
Lawton City	65	Cooke Co.[a]	126
Muskogee Co. & City[a,b]	300	Dawson Co.[a,b,j]	38
Nowata Co.	51	Denton Co.	1,209
Payne Co.	159	Fort Bend Co.[a,b]	887
Woods Co.	17	Freestone Co.	70
Oregon		Gregg Co.	727
Grant Co.	14	Hansford Co.	4
Linn Co.[a,b]	205	Hidalgo Co.	1,103
Malheur Co.	5	Hurst City[a]	26
Pennsylvania		Irving City	36
Clarion Co.	84	Jefferson Co.[a,b]	918
Clinton Co.[a,b]	293	Kerr Co.	157
Cumberland Co. Prison	399	Kimble Co.	13
Lebanon Co. Prison[b]	480	Lamar Co.	158
Luzerne Co. Corr. Fac.[a,b]	634	Maverick Co.	220
Monroe Co.[a]	395	McLennan Co.	1,025
Potter Co.	45	Midland Co.	306
South Carolina		Montgomery Co.[a,b]	1,037
Alvin S. Glenn Det. Ctr.[a]	944	Moore Co.	44
Chester Co.	87	Navarro Co.	186
Florence Co.	368	Ochiltree Co.	21
Greenville Co.	1,086	Oldham Co.	5
Greenwood Co.	167	Parker Co.[g]	392
Marion Co.[a,b,g,h,i]	139	Parmer Co.[a,b,g]	31
McCormick Co.[a]	12	Randall Co.	358
Spartanburg Co. Det. Fac.[c,d,f]	763	Red River Co.	34
Sumter-Lee Reg. Det. Ctr.	365	San Jacinto Co.	82
Union Co.	54	Schleicher Co.	8
South Dakota		Swisher Co.	16
Marshall Co.	1	Taylor Co.	544
Meade Co.	50	Terrell Co.[a]	2
Minnehaha Co.	510	Terry Co.	84
Walworth Co.	22	Tom Green Co.[a]	400
Tennessee		Uvalde Co.	43
Anderson Co.[c,d,e,f]	308	**Utah**	
Benton Co.	70	Cache Co.	290
Clay Co.	25	Carbon Co.	80
Hawkins Co.	185	Iron Co.[a]	135
Johnson City	104	Juab Co.[a]	35
Johnson Co.	132	Washington Co.[a,b,h]	468
Knox Co.	1,047	**Virginia**	
Montgomery Co.	373	Alexandria City[a,b]	250
Polk Co.[b,i]	140	Central Virginia Reg. Jail[b,h]	381
Robertson Co.	125	Franklin Co.[b]	60
Rutherford Co. Corr. Work Ctr.[b]	180	Middle River Reg. Jail[a,b]	551
Scott Co.[a]	129	Rappahannock Reg. Jail & Annex[a,b]	1,384
Sevier Co.[b,h]	470	Roanoke City	620
Warren Co.	253	Rockbridge Reg. Jail[b]	87
		Rockingham Co.	333

TABLE 7 (continued)
Local jail authorities with no allegations of sexual victimization, 2011

Jurisdiction and facility	Average daily population
Virginia (continued)	
Southampton Co.	96
Virginia Peninsula Reg. Jail[a,g]	409
Washington	
Chelan Co. Reg. Justice Ctr.	303
Clallam Co.[a,b]	114
Island Co.[a,b]	43
Puyallup City	36
Skamania Co.	25
West Virginia	
Potomac Highlands Reg. Jail	298
Southwestern Reg. Jail	431
Western Reg. Jail[g]	571
Wisconsin	
Ashland Co.[h]	57
Buffalo Co.	22
Eau Claire Co.	221
La Crosse Co.	172
Langlade Co.[a,b]	75
Rock Co.	468
Rusk Co.[a,b]	38
Waushara Co.	85
Winnebago Co.	289
Wyoming	
Albany Co.	46
Natrona Co. Det. Ctr.	270
Sublette Co.[a,b]	17

[a]Allegations of abusive sexual contact could not be counted separately from allegations of nonconsensual sexual acts.

[b]Allegations of staff sexual harassment could not be counted separately from allegations of staff sexual misconduct.

[c]Agency did not record allegations of nonconsensual sexual acts.

[d]Agency did not record allegations of abusive sexual contact.

[e]Agency did not record allegations of staff sexual misconduct.

[f]Agency did not record allegations of staff sexual harassment.

[g]Counts of nonconsensual sexual acts were based on substantiated allegations only.

[h]Counts of staff sexual misconduct were based on substantiated allegations only.

[i]Counts of nonconsensual sexual acts were based on completed acts only.

[j]Average daily population was unavailable; the Deaths in Custody Reporting Program population was used in its place.

Source: Bureau of Justice Statistics, Survey of Sexual Violence, 2011.

TABLE 8
Local jail authorities with no allegations of sexual victimization, 2010

Jurisdiction and facility	Average daily population	Jurisdiction and facility	Average daily population
Total	145,916	**Colorado**	
Alabama		Clear Creek Co.	117
Birmingham City	166	Delta Co.[a,b]	47
Blount Co. Corr. Fac.	140	Lincoln Co.	36
Citronelle City	3	Mesa Co.[a]	368
Coosa Co.	64	Montrose Co.[a,b]	99
De Kalb Co.[a,b]	286	Sedgwick Co.	1
Hartselle City[a,b,c,d]	8	Washington Co.	193
Homewood City	18	**Florida**	
Jefferson Co.	1,239	Charlotte Co.	521
Lauderdale Co.[a,b]	157	DeSoto Co.[a,b]	194
Lawrence Co.	118	Dixie Co.[a,b]	74
Montgomery City	324	Escambia Co.	1,501
Montgomery Co.	513	Glades Co.[a]	514
Opp City[a]	5	Hamilton Co.	64
St. Clair Co.[c]	280	Hardee Co.[a,b]	84
Tallapoosa Co.	176	Hendry Co.	231
Wilcox Co.	54	Highlands Co.[a]	408
Winston Co.	45	Holmes Co.[b,f]	105
Alaska		Lee Co.	1,766
Homer City	1	Leon Co. Det. Fac.	981
Kotzebue Reg. Jail[a]	13	Pinellas Co.	3,171
Arizona		Suwanee Co.	180
Apache Co.	90	**Georgia**	
La Paz Co. Adult Det. Fac.	174	Baldwin Co.	256
Mohave Co.	395	Barrow Co. Det. Ctr.[a,b]	255
Navajo Co.	334	Bartow Co.	626
Pinal Co.	1,204	Bibb Co.	933
Arkansas		Clarke Co.	359
Benton Co.[b]	478	Colquitt Co.	238
Crittenden Co.[a]	322	Crawford Co.[a]	16
Dallas Co.	103	Crisp Co.[a,b]	192
Faulkner Co.[c]	279	Decatur Co.[b]	153
Miller Co.[a,b]	220	Douglas Co.[a,b]	798
Randolph Co.	32	Early Co.	30
Saline Co. Det. Fac.[a,b,e]	165	Effingham Co.[a,b]	164
Sevier Co.[a]	48	Emanuel Co.[a,b]	110
Warren City[a,b]	3	Grovetown City	3
California		Gwinnett Co. Comprehensive Corr. Complex	497
Amador Co.[a,b]	92	Harris Co. Prison	106
Butte Co.[a,b]	548	Houston Co.[a]	495
Contra Costa Co.	1,725	Jackson Co. Corr. Inst.	199
Imperial Co.	544	Jones Co.	147
Kings Co.	317	Lamar Co.	130
Long Beach City	85	Lowndes Co.	670
Marin Co.	284	Lumpkin Co.	91
Sacramento Co.	3,987	Milledgeville City	9
San Benito Co.	126	Monroe Co.[a]	123
San Mateo Co.[a,b]	1,037	Murray Co.	128
Sierra Co.	4	Muscogee Co.	1,035
Solano Co.	850	Pierce Co.[a]	49
Tulare Co.	1,341	Putnam Co.	103
Yolo Co. Monroe Det. Ctr.	418	Richmond Co. Corr. Inst.	215
Yuba Co.	467	South Fulton Municipal Reg. Jail - Union City[a,g]	217
		Spalding Co.[a,b,c,h]	436
		Spalding Co. Prison[a,b,c,h]	378
		Terrell Co. Prison	136

TABLE 8 (continued)
Local jail authorities with no allegations of sexual victimization, 2010

Jurisdiction and facility	Average daily population	Jurisdiction and facility	Average daily population
Georgia (continued)		**Kansas**	
Thomas Co. Prison	188	Butler Co.	233
Troup Co. Prison	361	Crawford Co.a,b	83
Worth Co.a	40	Douglas Co.a	140
Idaho		Geary Co.	113
Bonner Co.	90	Haskell Co.	5
Clearwater Co.	23	Jackson Co.	68
Illinois		Jefferson Co.	22
Adams Co.a,c	110	Pratt Co.	19
Carroll Co.	18	Sherman Co.	7
Effingham Co.	62	Smith Co.	4
Knox Co.	106	Sumner Co. L.E. Ctr.	120
Lasalle Co.	169	**Kentucky**	
Lawrence Co.	20	Barren Co. Corr. Ctr.	149
Marshall Co.	7	Big Sandy Reg. Det. Ctr.	221
McDonough Co.	41	Boone Co.	497
Peoria Co.a,b	498	Bourbon Co. Det. Ctr.	123
Perry Co.h	56	Campbell Co. Dention Ctr.a,b	530
St. Clair Co.c	483	Casey Co. Det. Ctr.	300
Stephenson Co.	119	Clay Co. Det. Ctr.	275
Vermilion Co.	252	Grayson Co. Det. Ctr.	550
White Co.c,d	80	Harlan Co. Det. Ctr.a,b,c	214
Whiteside Co.	109	Herman Ford Det. Ctr.	144
Indiana		Larue Co. Det. Ctr.	145
Bartholomew Co.	162	Laurel Co. Det. Ctr.	343
Boone Co.	147	Lewis Co. Det. Ctr.a,b	72
Clinton Co.	174	McCracken Co. Reg. Jaila	440
Floyd Co.	294	Meade Co. Det. Ctr.	140
Hamilton Co.a,h	326	Powell Co.a,b	215
Jennings Co.	147	Rockcastle Co. Det. Ctr.	99
Lake Co.a	832	Todd Co. Det. Ctr.	109
Lawrence Co.	150	Wayne Co. Det. Ctr.	179
Madison Co.	250	**Louisiana**	
Marion Co.	1,134	Ascension Parish	446
Monroe Co.	245	Avoyelles Parish	1,225
Morgan Co.a,b	250	Beauregard Parish	179
Posey Co.e,f,h,i	54	Claiborne Parish Det. Fac.g	645
Pulaski Co.	108	East Baton Rouge Parish Prisonh	1,631
Randolph Co.	89	East Feliciana Parish Prison	146
Tippecanoe Co.a,b	503	Franklin Parish Det. Ctr.a,b	798
Vigo Co.a,c	287	Iberville Parish	115
White Co.	110	Jefferson Parish	1,069
Whitley Co.	161	La Salle Parish	12
Iowa		Lafourche Parish Det. Ctr.	205
Black Hawk Co.a,b	268	Madison Parish Det. Ctr.	880
Clinton Co.	42	Morehouse Parish	514
Hancock Co.	6	Opelousas City	69
Hardin Co.a	89	Sabine Parish Det. Ctr.a,b,i	139
Harrison Co.a	12	St. Bernard Parish Prison	265
Ida Co.	4	Tangipahoa Parish	525
Mahaska Co.a,b,g	18	Webster Parish	490
Marion Co.a	18	**Maine**	
Polk Co.	1,018	Oxford Co.	5
Pottawattamie Co.	237	Penobscot Co.a,b	166
Wayne Co.	10		

TABLE 8 (continued)
Local jail authorities with no allegations of sexual victimization, 2010

Jurisdiction and facility	Average daily population	Jurisdiction and facility	Average daily population
Maryland		**Missouri (continued)**	
Dorchester Co.	166	Phelps Co.[a,c,h]	133
Prince George's Co. Corr. Ctr.	1,093	St. Clair Co.[a,b]	98
Queen Anne's Co. Det. Ctr.[b]	91	Sullivan Co.	1
Somerset Co. Det. Ctr.	100	West Plains City[c]	1
Wicomico Co.[a,b,d]	502	Wright Co.[c,d,h]	24
Massachusetts		**Montana**	
Essex Co. Corr. Fac.[b]	1,211	Glacier Co.	16
Hampshire Co.[a,b]	278	Lincoln Co.	23
Worcester Co. Jail & House of Corr.[a,b]	1,450	Missoula Co.	307
Michigan		Wheatland Co.[a,b,g]	3
Branch Co.[a]	110	**Nebraska**	
Calhoun Co.[a]	539	Cherry Co.	8
Clinton Co.	183	Dawes Co.[a,b]	16
Gogebic Co.[a,b]	28	Dundy Co.	1
Iron Co.	35	Platte Co.[a,b,c,h]	95
Kent Co.[a]	1,075	Sarpy Co.[a]	147
Midland Co.	184	Valley Co.[b,h]	2
Newaygo Co.[a,b]	212	**Nevada**	
Osceola Co.	64	Henderson Det. Ctr.[b]	350
Ottawa Co.	330	Nye Co.[a,b]	3
St. Clair Co.	443	**New Hampshire**	
Van Buren Co.	97	Hillsborough Co. House of Corr.	587
Minnesota		**New Jersey**	
Anoka Co.	200	Burlington Co.	522
Beltrami Co.	102	Cape May Co.	244
Clay Co.[a]	74	Essex Co. Corr. Fac.	2,293
Hennepin Co. Adult Corr. Fac.	458	Mercer Co. Corr. Ctr.	813
Northwest Reg. Corr. Ctr.[a,b]	123	Passaic Co.	1,046
Olmstead Co.[a,c,h]	170	Warren Co. Dept. of Corr.	136
Rice Co.[a,b]	46	**New Mexico**	
Scott Co.	103	Artesia City	4
Sibley Co.	10	Eddy Co. Det. Ctr.	231
Steele Co. Det. Ctr.	72	Luna Co. Det. Ctr.[g]	394
Wadena Co.	21	McKinley Co.[d]	220
Mississippi		Roosevelt Co. Det. Ctr.[a]	95
Choctaw Co.	31	**New York**	
Coahoma Co.	69	Albany Co.	720
Hinds Co.[a]	1,075	Chemung Co.[a]	181
Holmes-Humphreys Co. Reg. Corr. Fac.	319	Oneida Co.	448
Jefferson Davis Co.	35	Onondaga Co. Justice Ctr.[a]	621
Kemper-Neshoba Co. Reg. Corr. Fac.	343	Rensselaer Co.	228
Lafayette Co.	160	Saratoga Co.	171
Panola Co.	121	Schoharie Co.[a,b]	45
Stone Co. Reg. Corr. Fac.	404	St. Lawrence Co.	139
Webster Co.[a,b]	10	Suffolk Co.	1,732
Winston-Choctaw Reg. Corr. Fac.	278	Tioga Co.	83
Missouri		Ulster Co.	334
Bates Co.	100	Warren Co.[a]	155
Boone Co.	220	Washington Co.	118
Cape Giradeau Co.	189	**North Carolina**	
Chariton Co.	13	Bladen Co.[a]	81
Clark Co.	17	Brunswick Co.[h]	266
Maries Co.	12	Buncombe Co.	465
Morgan Co.	118	Burke Co.[f]	41
Pemiscot Co.	85	Carteret Co.	128
		Caswell Co.	1,241

TABLE 8 (continued)
Local jail authorities with no allegations of sexual victimization, 2010

Jurisdiction and facility	Average daily population	Jurisdiction and facility	Average daily population
North Carolina (continued)		**Pennsylvania (continued)**	
Cumberland Co.[a,b]	588	Fayette Co. Prison[a,b,d]	305
Durham Co. Det. Ctr.[a,b]	583	Jefferson Co.[a]	110
Iredell Co.	337	Lancaster Co. Prison[a]	1,148
Jones Co.[a,b,c]	23	Lawrence Co. Corr.	229
Lee Co.	101	Mifflin Co.	99
Lincoln Co.	131	Potter Co.	26
Montgomery Co.[a]	80	Snyder Co. Prison	97
Nash Co.	232	**South Carolina**	
Onslow Co.[a]	199	Bamberg Co.[a]	27
Pasquotank Co.[a]	127	Cherokee Co.[c,h]	165
Person Co.[a]	104	Chesterfield Co.	92
Rutherford Co.	153	Darlington Co.[a]	237
Vance Co.	171	Florence Co.	351
Wake Co.[a,b]	1,353	Horry Co.[a,b]	635
Wayne Co.	227	Jasper Co.[h]	172
North Dakota		Lancaster Co.	150
Cass Co.[g]	200	Orangeburg Calhoun Original Det. Ctr.	292
Ohio		Pickens Co. Prison	91
Ashtabula Co.	58	Sumter-Lee Reg. Det. Ctr.[a]	363
Butler Co.	922	**South Dakota**	
Clark Co.	203	Brule Co.[a]	12
Fayette Co.	40	Codington Co.[c]	56
Franklin Co. Comm. Based Corr. Fac.[a,b]	184	Minnehaha Co.	518
Lake Co.	313	**Tennessee**	
Lawrence Co.[g]	70	Bradley Co.[a,b]	388
Mayfield Heights City	1	Coffee Co.	311
Medina Co.	187	Decatur Co.	24
Multi-Co. Corr. Ctr.	173	Dickson Co.	245
Noble Co.[a,b]	18	Franklin Co.	130
Shelby Co.	78	Gibson Co.	150
Washington Co.[a]	113	Grainger Co.	91
Wood Co. Justice Ctr.	144	Hamilton Co.[a]	513
Oklahoma		Macon Co.[h]	125
Beckham Co.[a,b,g]	100	Marshall Co.	56
Carnegie City	5	Monroe Co.	188
Carter Co.[a,b]	165	Overton Co.	151
Comanche Co. Det. Ctr.[a,b]	283	Scott Co.	138
Grady Co.	545	Shelby Co. Govt. Div. of Corr.	2,600
Grant Co.	31	Tipton Co.	135
Kay Co. Det. Ctr.	145	Unicoi Co.	55
Logan Co.[a,c]	154	Weakley Co.	87
McClain Co.	63	Williamson Co.	271
Murray Co.	42	**Texas**	
Sequoyah Co.[a]	108	Bastrop Co.	326
Tillman Co.	89	Bee Co.	100
Oregon		Brooks Co.	24
Douglas Co.	224	Cameron Co.	1,267
Klamath Co.[a]	84	Cass Co.	119
Malheur Co.[g]	88	Coryell Co.[a,b]	81
Polk Co.	142	Crockett Co.	0
Pennsylvania		Dallam Co.	35
Allegheny Co.[a,b]	2,672	Dawson Co.[b]	36
Armstrong Co.[a,b,e]	151	Denton Co.	1,199
Beaver Co.	340	Dewitt Co.	80
Bedford Co. Prison	165	El Paso Co.[a,b]	2,103
Blair Co. Prison[a,b]	281	Fannin Co.[a]	366
Cambria Co.	486		

TABLE 8 (continued)
Local jail authorities with no allegations of sexual victimization, 2010

Jurisdiction and facility	Average daily population	Jurisdiction and facility	Average daily population
Texas (continued)		**Washington**	
Hardin Co.	159	Asotin Co.[f,i]	54
Harrison Co.	173	Clallam Co.[a,b]	119
Henderson Co.	304	Franklin Co.[a,b]	178
Hidalgo Co.	1,217	Grays Harbor Co.	142
Hill Co.	147	Olympia City	47
Hood Co.[c]	165	Skagit Co.	243
Jefferson Co.	910	**West Virginia**	
Keller City[a,b]	2	Bluefield City	5
Kleberg Co.[g]	100	McDowell Co.[a]	4
Matagorda Co.[a,b]	177	Western Reg. Jail[c,d,h]	538
Menard Co.	5	**Wisconsin**	
Midland Co.	335	Barron Co. Justice Ctr.[a,b]	130
Montgomery Co.	978	Fond du Lac Co.[a,b]	295
San Patricio Co.	194	La Crosse Co.	173
Scurry Co.[a,b]	48	Langlade Co.	85
Shelby Co.[c,d,h]	55	Oneida Co.	156
Swisher Co.	15	Outagamie Co.	365
Tarrant Co.[a,b]	3,149	Ozaukee Co.	223
Taylor Co.[c]	490	Racine Co.	702
Tom Green Co.	412	Richland Co.[a,b]	33
Van Zandt Co.	155	Sauk Co.	228
Washington Co.	107	Sawyer Co.	77
Williamson Co.	651	St. Croix Co.	96
Winkler Co.[a,b]	90	**Wyoming**	
Utah		Natrona Co. Det. Ctr.[a,b]	293
Box Elder Co.[a,b]	122	Park Co.[a]	63
Juab Co.	30		
San Juan Co.	87		
Washington Co.[a,b,h]	471		
Virginia			
Albemarle Charlottesville Reg. Jail	458		
Appomattox Co.	29		
Blue Ridge Reg. Jail	1,014		
Botetourt Co.	85		
Central Virginia Reg. Jail	356		
Chesapeake City	1,037		
Chesterfield Co.	318		
Fauquier Co.	110		
Henry Co.	170		
Loudoun Co.[a,b]	193		
Newport News Dept. of Adult Corr.[a]	148		
Peumansend Creek Reg. Jail[a]	213		
Pittsylvania Co.	119		
Portsmouth	418		
Prince William - Manassas Reg. Adult Det.	860		
Rappahannock Reg. Jail & Annex[a,b]	1,387		
Richmond City	1,402		
Southampton Co.	84		

[a]Allegations of abusive sexual contact could not be counted separately from allegations of nonconsensual sexual acts.

[b]Allegations of staff sexual harassment could not be counted separately from allegations of staff sexual misconduct.

[c]Counts of nonconsensual sexual acts were based on substantiated allegations only.

[d]Counts of nonconsensual sexual acts were based on completed acts only.

[e]Agency did not record allegations of nonconsensual sexual acts.

[f]Agency did not record allegations of abusive sexual contact.

[g]Average daily population was unavailable; the Deaths in Custody Reporting Program population was used in its place.

[h]Counts of staff sexual misconduct were based on substantiated allegations only.

[i]Agency did not record allegations of staff sexual harassment.

Source: Bureau of Justice Statistics, Survey of Sexual Violence, 2010.

TABLE 9
Local jail authorities with no allegations of sexual victimization, 2009

Jurisdiction and facility	Average daily population	Jurisdiction and facility	Average daily population
Total	131,655	**Colorado**	
Alabama		Adams Co. Det. Fac.	1,298
Arab City	14	Arapahoe Co.	1,057
Baldwin Co. Corr. Ctr.	600	Clear Creek Co.[b,c]	90
Barbour Co.[a]	100	Delta Co.	63
Clarke Co.	100	El Paso Co.	1,499
Coffee Co.	158	Lincoln Co.[b,c]	29
Colbert Co.	76	Montezuma Co.	118
Covington Co.	198	Montrose Co.	165
De Kalb Co.[b]	280	Morgan Co. Det.	95
Fayette Co.	48	**Florida**	
Jackson Co.	130	Collier Co. Det. Ctr.	881
Jefferson Co.	1,100	Flagler Inmate Fac.	138
Lamar Co.	60	Glades Co.	538
Limestone Co.[b]	234	Hendry Co.[a,b,c,e]	233
Marshall Co.	255	Hillsborough Co.[b]	3,461
Midfield City	3	Lafayette Co.	20
Pickens Co.	107	Leon Co. Det. Fac.	991
Russell Co.	308	Liberty Co.	56
Satsuma City	7	Marion Co.[b,c]	1,648
Walker Co.	173	Monroe Co.	593
Alaska		Suwanee Co.	170
Bristol Bay Borough	1	Taylor Co.	108
Arizona		Washington Co.	120
Cochise Co.	241	**Georgia**	
Pinal Co.[b]	1,196	Athens-Clarke Co. Corr. Inst.[b,c]	107
Santa Cruz Co.[b]	103	Augusta-Richmond Co.	1,006
Arkansas		Barrow Co. Det. Ctr.	247
Benton Co.[b,c]	492	Ben Hill Co.	104
Clay Co.	97	Brantley Co.	91
Garland Co. Criminal Det. Fac.	217	Butts Co. Det. Ctr.	175
Lawrence Co.	42	Carroll Co. Prison	225
Lincoln Co.	17	Clarke Co.	370
Miller Co.	275	Cobb Co. Jail & Prison	2,385
Montgomery Co.	10	Colquitt Co. Prison[b,c]	177
Pope Co. Det. Ctr.[b]	178	Coweta Co. Prison & Corr. Inst.	202
Pulaski Co. Reg. Jail	998	Dawson Co.	183
Saline Co. Det. Fac.	317	Dooly Co.	141
St. Francis Co.	85	Fannin Co.	64
White Co. Det. Ctr.	179	Forsyth Co.	353
California		Fulton Co.[b]	2,846
Glendale City	14	Glynn Co. Det. Ctr.	470
Glenn Co.	95	Gordon Co.	275
Lake Co. Hill Road Corr. Fac.[c,d]	230	Hall Co. Det. Ctr.	1,128
Long Beach City	98	Haralson Co.	82
Marin Co.	267	Irwin Co. Det. Ctr.[b,c]	670
Mendocino Co.	283	Jackson Co.	157
Monterey Co.	1,004	Jefferson Co.[b,c]	201
San Mateo Co.[b,c]	1,107	Jones Co.	154
Stanislaus Co.	1,322	Lowndes Co.	698
Tulare Co.	1,530	Mcintosh Co.[b,c]	100
Tuolumne Co.[b]	141	Milledgeville City	4
Yolo Co. Monroe Det. Ctr.[b,c]	449	Murray Co.	105
		Muscogee Co. Prison	572
		Pickens Co.	71
		Pike Co.	59
		Polk Co.[b,c]	208

TABLE 9 (continued)
Local jail authorities with no allegations of sexual victimization, 2009

Jurisdiction and facility	Average daily population	Jurisdiction and facility	Average daily population
Georgia (continued)		**Kansas (continued)**	
Putnam Co.	87	Lyon Co.	135
Rabun Co. Det. Ctr.	79	Miami Co.	42
Rockdale Co.	485	Russell Co.	16
South Fulton Municipal Reg. Jail - Union City[b,c]	323	Smith Co.	1
Stephens Co.	179	Sumner Co. L.E. Ctr.	90
Sumter Co. Prison	342	Woodson Co.	2
Upson Co.[b]	173	**Kentucky**	
Walker Co.[b,c]	203	Barren Co. Corr. Ctr.	120
Idaho		Boone Co.[b]	405
Bingham Co.	104	Bourbon Co. Det. Ctr.[e]	110
Nez Perce Det. Fac.[b]	56	Casey Co. Det. Ctr.	265
Oneida Co.[b,c,f]	270	Christian Co.[b]	631
Illinois		Clark Co. Det.	177
De Kalb Co.	118	Crittenden Co. Det. Ctr.	101
Jefferson Co. Justice Ctr.[b,e,g]	180	Henderson Co. Det. Ctr.[c,e,g]	540
Macon Co.	245	Larue Co. Det. Ctr.	156
Mason Co.	45	Mason Co.	143
St. Clair Co.	311	Meade Co. Det. Ctr.	143
Stephenson Co.[b]	164	Muhlenberg Co. Det. Ctr.[b]	269
Wayne Co.	24	Nelson Co.	129
White Co.	70	Rockcastle Co. Det. Ctr.[c]	98
Whiteside Co.	109	Simpson Co. Det. Ctr.[c]	205
Williamson Co.[b]	97	Three Forks Reg. Det. Ctr.[b,c]	214
Indiana		Webster Co. Det. Ctr.[c]	104
Allen Co.	790	**Louisiana**	
Boone Co.[b]	144	Amite City[b,c]	8
Cass Co.	171	Avoyelles Parish	1,218
Clay Co.	125	Concordia Parish Corr. Fac.	510
Daviess Co. Security Ctr.	194	De Soto Parish	91
Jackson Co.	187	East Feliciana Parish Prison	200
Johnson Co.	304	Iberville Parish	128
Knox Co.	188	Jackson Parish Corr. Ctr.	823
Kosciusko Co.[e]	239	Madison Parish Det. Ctr.	1,074
Morgan Co.[b,c]	230	Madison Parish Jail[e]	33
Randolph Co.	87	Natchitoches Det. Ctr.[b,g]	438
Ripley Co.	99	Shreveport City	132
Starke Co.[e]	69	St. Bernard Parish Prison[e]	260
Tipton Co.	36	St. Landry Parish	236
Wayne Co.	324	Vermilion Parish L.E. Ctr.	142
White Co.	122	Vernon Parish Corr. Fac.[h,i]	200
Whitley Co.	154	**Maine**	
Iowa		Penobscot Co.	168
Clay Co.	8	Washington Co.	37
Hardin Co.	85	York Co.	228
Keokuk Co.	6	**Maryland**	
Lucas Co.[b]	5	Cecil Co. Det. Ctr.	181
Lyon Co.	18	Charles Co. Det. Ctr.	392
O'Brien Co.[b,c]	29	Garrett Co.	46
Polk Co.	1,060	Kent Co. Det. Ctr.	84
Pottawattamie Co.	204	Queen Anne's Co. Det. Ctr.	96
Scott Co.	258	Worcester Co.	175
Kansas		**Massachusetts**	
Finney Co.	126	Essex Co. Corr. Fac.	842
Harvey Co. Det. Ctr.[a]	100	Plymouth Co. House of Corr.[b]	1,272
Jackson Co.[b]	87		
Leavenworth Co.	109		

TABLE 9 (continued)
Local jail authorities with no allegations of sexual victimization, 2009

Jurisdiction and facility	Average daily population	Jurisdiction and facility	Average daily population
Michigan		**Montana**	
Alger Co.[b,c]	15	Lake Co.[b]	36
Arenac Co.[b]	37	Musselshell Co.	6
Chippewa Co.	116	Roosevelt Co.	12
Clare Co.[c]	167	Yellowstone Co. Det. Fac.[b]	350
Delta Co.	95	**Nebraska**	
Grand Traverse Co.[b]	137	Dakota Co.[b]	105
Isabella Co.[b,c]	206	Holt Co.	300
Kent Co.	1,131	Kearney Co.[b,c]	2
Lapeer Co.	137	Platte Co.[b,g]	116
Midland Co.[b,c]	110	Seward Co.	22
Monroe Co.	325	**Nevada**	
Newaygo Co.	210	Henderson Det. Ctr.	263
Osceola Co.	65	Nye Co.	4
Saginaw Co.[b]	487	**New Hampshire**	
Van Buren Co.	143	Belknap Co.	99
Minnesota		Cheshire Co.	112
Anoka Co.	211	**New Jersey**	
Anoka Co. Work Release #1 & 4	131	Atlantic Co.[b]	1,015
Brown Co.	27	Mercer Co. Corr. Ctr.	1,030
Carver Co.	85	**New Mexico**	
Goodhue Co.	97	Chaves Co. Det. Ctr.[b,c]	217
Hennepin Co. Adult Det. Ctr.	694	Dona Ana Co. Det. Ctr.[b]	818
Isanti Co.	63	Luna Co. Det. Ctr.	263
Stearns Co.	193	Quay Co. Det. Ctr.	37
Washington Co.	200	**New York**	
Watonwan Co.	12	Cayuga Co.	203
Mississippi		Chemung Co.	190
Carroll-Montgomery Co. Reg. Corr. Ctr.[a,e,g]	317	Chenango Co.	66
Chickasaw Co.	82	Columbia Co.	105
Claiborne Co.[b,c]	2	Cortland Co.[a,e]	63
Coahoma Co.	100	Dutchess Co.[b,c]	344
Humphreys Co.	31	Madison Co.	107
Jefferson-Franklin Co. Corr. Fac.	277	Monroe Co.	1,439
Lincoln Co.	80	Montgomery Co.[g]	107
Marion-Walthall Co. Reg. Corr. Fac.	100	Ontario Co.	222
Monroe Co.[b]	91	Wayne Co.[b,c]	116
Panola Co.	104	**North Carolina**	
Tishomingo Co.	32	Buncombe Co.	431
Missouri		Duplin Co.	119
Barton Co.[c,e]	20	Franklin Co. Det. Ctr.[b,c]	132
Bates Co.	100	Halifax Co.	124
Boone Co.	200	Harnett Co.	161
Cape Giradeau Co.	184	Hertford Co.	98
Cole Co.	48	Iredell Co.	324
Daviess-Dekalb Reg. Jail	170	Johnston Co.[b]	202
Franklin Co.	123	McDowell Co.	99
Lafayette Co.[b,c]	96	Mecklenburg Co.	2,846
Mississippi Co.	100	New Hanover Det. Fac.	474
Moniteau Co.	12	Pender Co.	78
Pemiscot Co.	104	Richmond Co.[b]	90
Platte Co.	95	Rockingham Co.	180
St. Louis City	1,296	Transylvania Co.	42
Ste. Genevieve Co.[g]	110	Vance Co.	179
Stone Co. L.E. Ctr.	45	Wake Co.	1,335
Warren Co.	98	Wayne Co.	212
West Plains City[b,c]	1	Wilson Co.	190

TABLE 9 (continued)
Local jail authorities with no allegations of sexual victimization, 2009

Jurisdiction and facility	Average daily population	Jurisdiction and facility	Average daily population
North Dakota		**South Carolina**	
Bottineau Co.	5	Alvin S. Glenn Det. Ctr.	992
Burleigh Co. Det. Ctr.	122	Berkely Co.	375
Cass Co.	201	Charleston Co.[b,c]	1,728
Ohio		Chester Co.[b]	113
Allen Co.	217	Darlington Co.	214
Ashtabula Co.	80	Dillon Co.[d,f]	175
Butler Co.	950	Lancaster Co.	173
Crawford Co.	101	Marion Co.	95
Delaware Co.[b]	152	Newberry Co.	187
Fairfield Co.	169	Sumter-Lee Reg. Det. Ctr.	403
Greene Co.	256	Williamsburg Co.[b]	96
Harrison Co.	8	York Co. Prison	154
Huron Co.	91	**South Dakota**	
Logan Co.[b]	56	Day Co.	5
Miami Co.[b]	89	Meade Co.	45
Muskingum Co.	163	**Tennessee**	
Pickaway Co.	131	Bedford Co.	100
Portage Co.	212	Bradley Co.	362
Richland Co.	229	Carroll Co.[b]	87
Summit Co. & Glenwood Annex	697	Cheatham Co.[c]	135
Wayne Co.	112	Chester Co.[b,c]	36
Zanesville City	40	Cocke Co.	60
Oklahoma		De Kalb Co.	80
Adair Co.	70	Dickson Co.[b,c]	242
Carter Co.	201	Franklin Co.	129
Checotah City	3	Grainger Co.	83
Custer Co.	120	Henry Co.[b,c]	165
Garfield Co.	269	Johnson Co.	97
Harmon Co.	7	Knox Co.	1,070
Kay Co. Det. Ctr.[c]	129	Marion Co.[b]	76
Le Flore Co. Det. Ctr.	155	Monroe Co.[a,b,c,e,g]	191
Lincoln Co.[b]	55	Obion Co.[b,c]	144
Okfuskee Co.[b,e]	34	Overton Co.	144
Ottawa Co.[b]	132	Robertson Co.	226
Rogers Co.[e]	198	Sequarchie Co.[b,c]	88
Wagoner Co.	98	Williamson Co.	301
Oregon		**Texas**	
Columbia Co.[b]	110	Aransas Co.	192
Harney Co.[b,c]	14	Bastrop Co.[b,c]	315
Klamath Co.[b]	123	Bee Co.[b,c]	104
Northern Oregon Reg. Corr. Fac.[c]	105	Bell Co.	632
Pennsylvania		Brazoria Co.	870
Blair Co. Prison[b,c]	289	Caldwell Co.	185
Clearfield Co. Prison	112	Cochran Co.	5
Fayette Co. Prison	234	Coleman Co.[b]	7
Greene Co. Prison[b,c]	82	Denton Co.	1,181
Lackawanna Co. Prison	920	Fannin Co.[b]	330
Lawrence Co. Corr.	196	Guadalupe Co.	479
Mifflin Co.	118	Harrison Co.	180
Montgomery Co.	1,768	Hill Co.	149
Pike Co.[b,c,g]	321	Hood Co.[c]	166
Union Co.	51	Hopkins Co.[b,c,g]	79
Venango Co.[b,c]	147	Hutchinson Co.	57
Warren Co. Prison[b,c]	115	Kaufman Co.	289
Wayne Co.	94	Kerr Co.	144
Westmoreland Co. Prison[b,c]	506	Kinney Co.[b,c,g]	23

TABLE 9 (continued)
Local jail authorities with no allegations of sexual victimization, 2009

Jurisdiction and facility	Average daily population	Jurisdiction and facility	Average daily population
Texas (continued)		**Washington**	
Kleberg Co.[j]	95	Ferry Co.[b]	30
Matagorda Co.[b,c]	163	Kittitas Co. Corr. Ctr.[b,c]	122
Menard Co.[b,c]	5	Mason Co.	109
Milam Co.	122	Okanogan Co.	162
Montague Co.	69	Olympia City	47
Morris Co.	28	Spokane Co.	559
Nacogdoches Co.[b,c]	208	**Wisconsin**	
Orange Co.[b,c]	192	Adams Co.[b,c]	67
Shelby Co.[g]	51	Barron Co. Justice Ctr.	105
Starr Co.	224	Jefferson Co.	176
Tarrant Co.[b]	3,175	Langlade Co.	97
Van Zandt Co.[c]	154	Manitowoc Co.[b,c]	168
Washington Co.[j]	104	Marathon Co. Adult Det. Fac.	280
Webb Co.	480	Milwaukee Co. Corr. Fac. So. (formerly House of Corr.)	1,938
Wise Co.	180	Oneida Co.	172
Wood Co.	79	Pierce Co.	27
Utah		Sauk Co.	268
Box Elder Co.	127	Washington Co.	255
Cache Co.[c]	300	Waukesha Co.	642
Emery Co.	37	Waupaca Co.	180
San Juan Co.	87	**Wyoming**	
Sevier Co.	106	Natrona Co. Det. Ctr.[b,c]	295
Utah Co.	726	Sheridan Co.[b,c]	115
Virginia		Washakie Co. Det. Ctr.	16
Accomack Co.[b]	98		
Amherst Co.	77		
Bristol City[b]	123		
Brunswick Co.	55		
Central Virginia Reg. Jail	451		
Danville City[b]	244		
Fairfax Co. Adult Det. Ctr.	1,354		
Middle Penninsula Reg. Security Ctr.	199		
Montgomery Co.	116		
Pittsylvania Co.	132		
Rappahannock Reg. Jail & Annex[c]	1,206		
Roanoke Co.	170		
Shenandoah Co.	107		
Virginia Beach City[b,c]	1,370		
Warren Co.[b]	127		

[a]Counts of nonconsensual sexual acts were based on completed acts only.

[b]Allegations of abusive sexual contact could not be counted separately from allegations of nonconsensual sexual acts.

[c]Allegations of staff sexual harassment could not be counted separately from allegations of staff sexual misconduct.

[d]Agency did not record allegations of abusive sexual contact.

[e]Counts of nonconsensual sexual acts were based on substantiated allegations only.

[f]Agency did not record allegations of nonconsensual sexual acts.

[g]Counts of staff sexual misconduct were based on substantiated allegations only.

[h]Agency did not record allegations of staff sexual misconduct.

[i]Agency did not record allegations of staff sexual harassment.

[j]Average daily population was unavailable; the Deaths in Custody Reporting Program population was used in its place.

Source: Bureau of Justice Statistics, Survey of Sexual Violence, 2009.

Section 3. Privately operated prisons and jails

TABLE 10
Allegations of sexual victimization reported by privately operated jail and prison authorities, by type of victimization, 2011

Jurisdiction and facility	Average daily population	Inmate-on-inmate				Staff-on-inmate			
		Nonconsensual sexual acts		Abusive sexual contact		Sexual misconduct		Sexual harassment	
		Alleged	Substantiated	Alleged	Substantiated	Alleged	Substantiated	Alleged	Substantiated
Total	75,579	110	6	84	16	151	19	66	15
Alaska									
Northstar Ctr. (GEO)[a]	130	0	0	/	/	1	0	1	0
Arizona									
Arizona State Prison - Florence West (GEO)	713	0	0	2	1	1	0	0	0
Arizona State Prison - Kingman (MTC)	2,907	2	0	0	0	0	0	0	0
Arizona State Prison - Phoenix West (GEO)	492	0	0	0	0	1	0	0	0
Eloy Det. Ctr. (CCA)	1,479	1	0	3	0	3	1	2	1
Tucson Res. Reentry Ctr. (Behavioral Systems Southwest)[a,b]	44	0	0	/	/	0	0	1	1
California									
California City Corr. Ctr. (CCA)	1,428	0	0	0	0	1	1	0	0
Colorado									
Bent Co. Corr. Fac. (CCA)	1,324	2	1	0	0	2	2	0	0
Cheyenne Mountain Reentry Ctr. (CEC)	657	1	0	1	0	4	0	0	0
Crowley Co. Corr. Fac. (CCA)	1,602	0	0	2	0	0	0	0	0
Kit Carson Co. Corr. Ctr. (CCA)	798	2	0	2	0	0	0	1	0
Pueblo Comm. Corr. Svs., Inc.	75	0	0	0	0	1	1	0	0
Florida									
Bay Co. (CCA)	861	1	0	0	0	0	0	0	0
Bay Corr. Inst. (CCA)	979	0	0	2	0	1	0	0	0
Citrus C (CCA)	566	0	0	3	2	2	0	4	1
Gadsden Corr. Fac. (MTC)	1,539	3	0	0	0	8	0	0	0
Lake City Corr. Fac. (CCA)	887	4	0	2	1	3	0	0	0
South Bay Corr. Fac. (GEO)[a]	1,856	0	0	/	/	0	0	2	1
Georgia									
Coffee Corr. Fac. (CCA)[b]	2,717	37	0	14	0	23	0	/	/
D. Ray James Prison (GEO)	2,235	1	0	0	0	0	0	0	0
McRae Corr. Fac. (CCA)	1,738	0	0	0	0	0	0	1	0
Wheeler Corr. Fac. (CCA)	2,780	0	0	1	0	0	0	3	0
Idaho									
Idaho Corr. Fac. (CCA)	2,004	3	2	1	0	0	0	1	0
Kentucky									
Lee Adjustment Ctr. (CCA)	448	1	0	1	0	2	0	1	0
Marion Adjustment Ctr. (CCA)	811	1	0	4	1	6	2	1	1
Otter Creek Corr. Complex (CCA)	637	1	0	2	1	8	0	0	0
Louisiana									
Allen Corr. Ctr. (GEO)	1,469	1	0	1	1	0	0	0	0
Winn Corr. Ctr. (CCA)	1,469	1	0	7	2	3	0	18	1
Massachusetts									
Coolidge House	101	0	0	0	0	1	0	0	0
Mississippi									
Marshall Co.Corr. Fac. (GEO)[a]	973	1	0	/	/	2	2	3	2
Tallahatchie Co. Corr. Fac. (CCA)	2,606	0	0	0	0	1	0	0	0
Walnut Grove Corr. Fac. (GEO)[a,b]	1,050	3	0	/	/	0	0	/	/
Wilkinson Co. Corr. Ctr. (CCA)	889	1	0	1	0	1	0	1	0
Montana									
Crossroads Corr. Ctr. (CCA)	631	2	0	2	1	7	0	0	0

TABLE 10 (continued)
Allegations of sexual victimization reported by privately operated jail and prison authorities, by type of victimization, 2011

Jurisdiction and facility	Average daily population	Inmate-on-inmate				Staff-on-inmate			
		Nonconsensual sexual acts		Abusive sexual contact		Sexual misconduct		Sexual harassment	
		Alleged	Substantiated	Alleged	Substantiated	Alleged	Substantiated	Alleged	Substantiated
New Mexico									
Cibola Co. Corr. Ctr. (CCA)	1,175	0	0	2	1	0	0	0	0
Guadalupe Co. Corr. Fac. (GEO)	554	2	1	0	0	1	0	0	0
Lea Co. Corr. Fac. (GEO)[a,b]	1,102	0	0	/	/	1	1	/	/
New Mexico Women's Corr. Fac. (CCA)	602	0	0	1	0	23	0	0	0
Torrance Co. Det. Fac. (CCA)	843	0	0	0	0	2	0	0	0
North Carolina									
Rivers Corr. Inst. (GEO)	1,400	0	0	2	0	0	0	0	0
Ohio									
Fannie M. Lewis Comm. Corr. & Treatment Ctr. (Oriana House, Inc.)[a]	194	1	0	/	/	0	0	0	0
Northeast Ohio Corr. Ctr. (CCA)	2,013	0	0	2	0	2	0	1	0
Oklahoma									
Carver Corr. Ctr.[a,b]	276	1	0	0	0	1	0	/	/
Cimarron Corr. Fac. (CCA)	649	2	0	6	1	2	0	5	1
David L. Moss Criminal Justice Ctr. (Tulsa Co., CCA)	1,614	1	1	4	1	0	0	0	0
Davis Corr. Fac. (CCA)	1,592	5	1	2	1	2	1	3	1
Lawton Corr. Fac. (GEO)	2,478	8	0	3	0	1	0	0	0
Pennsylvania									
Capitol Pavilion Comm. Corr. Ctr. (CEC)[a,b]	90	0	0	/	/	1	0	/	/
George W. Hill Corr. Fac. (CEC)[a]	1,876	4	0	/	/	0	0	0	0
Joseph Coleman Ctr.	283	1	0	0	0	0	0	0	0
Tennessee									
Hardeman Co. (CCA)	1,966	7	0	1	0	6	1	2	0
Metro-Davidson Co. Det. Fac. (CCA)	1,116	1	0	1	0	1	0	0	0
Silverdale Corr. Fac. (CCA)	842	2	0	4	1	3	1	7	2
South Central Corr. Ctr. (CCA)	1,630	3	0	1	0	6	0	2	0
Whiteville Corr. Fac. (CCA)	1,493	2	0	3	1	5	0	3	1
Texas									
Dalby Corr. Ctr. (MTC)	1,903	0	0	0	0	1	1	0	0
Eden Corr. Ctr. (CCA)	1,548	0	0	0	0	3	0	1	0
Houston-Reid Ctr. (GEO)	505	0	0	1	0	0	0	0	0
Liberty Co. (CEC)	118	0	0	0	0	2	1	0	0
Reeves Co., Complex 2 (GEO)	2,374	0	0	0	0	3	3	2	2
Reeves Co., Det. Complex R1, R2, & R3 (GEO)	1,335	0	0	0	0	1	0	0	0
Riverside Treatment Ctr. (VOA)[a]	89	0	0	/	/	1	0	0	0
Val Verde Corr. Fac. & Co. Jail	1,452	0	0	0	0	1	1	0	0
Virginia									
Lawrenceville Corr. Ctr. (GEO)	1,572	1	0	0	0	0	0	0	0

CCA - Corrections Corp. of America

CEC - Community Education Centers, Inc.

GEO - The GEO Group, Inc.

MTC - Management & Training Corp.

VOA - Volunteers of America

/ Not reported.

[a]Allegations of abusive sexual contact could not be counted separately from allegations of nonconsensual sexual acts.

[b]Allegations of staff sexual harassment could not be counted separately from allegations of staff sexual misconduct.

Source: Bureau of Justice Statistics, Survey of Sexual Violence, 2011.

TABLE 11
Allegations of sexual victimization reported by privately operated jail and prison authorities, by type of victimization, 2010

Jurisdiction and facility	Average daily population	Inmate-on-inmate				Staff-on-inmate			
		Nonconsensual sexual acts		Abusive sexual contact		Sexual misconduct		Sexual harassment	
		Alleged	Substantiated	Alleged	Substantiated	Alleged	Substantiated	Alleged	Substantiated
Total	68,740	99	7	55	6	89	13	51	6
Arizona									
Arizona State Prison - Kingman (MTC)[a]	2,159	1	0	0	0	0	0	/	/
Eloy Det. Ctr. (CCA)	1,490	3	0	4	0	0	0	0	0
California									
California City Corr. Ctr. (CCA)	1,711	1	0	0	0	0	0	1	0
Desert View Modified Comm. Corr. Fac. (GEO)	620	0	0	0	0	0	0	1	0
Vinewood Comm. Corr. (CA DOC)[a,b,c]	61	0	0	/	/	1	1	/	/
Colorado									
Bent Co. Corr. Fac. (CCA)	1,376	0	0	0	0	0	0	2	1
Crowley Co. Corr. Fac. (CCA)	1,650	0	0	1	1	3	1	0	0
Kit Carson Co. Corr. Ctr. (CCA)[c]	823	2	0	/	/	1	1	1	0
Florida									
Bay Corr. Inst. (CCA)	979	0	0	0	0	2	0	0	0
Citrus C (CCA)	570	0	0	1	1	0	0	0	0
Gadsden Corr. Fac. (MTC, CCA)[d]	1,525	1	0	1	0	4	1	3	0
South Bay Corr. Fac. (GEO)[c]	1,858	2	0	/	/	0	0	0	0
Georgia									
Coffee Corr. Fac. (CCA)	2,241	3	0	3	0	0	0	5	1
D. Ray James Prison (GEO)[d]	2,017	2	0	5	0	3	0	5	0
Dismas House - Atlanta Community Corr. Ctr. (DC)	530	4	0	0	0	3	0	0	0
McRae Corr. Fac. (CCA)	1,740	0	0	1	0	1	0	0	0
Wheeler Corr. Fac. (CCA)	2,214	2	0	1	0	0	0	0	0
Idaho									
Idaho Corr. Fac. (CCA)	2,031	6	0	0	0	4	1	0	0
Illinois									
Substance Abuse Svs. (The H Group)	52	0	0	0	0	0	0	1	1
Indiana									
Marion Co. Jail II (CCA)	1,022	1	0	1	0	0	0	0	0
Kansas									
Leavenworth (CCA)	854	5	0	0	0	0	0	3	0
Kentucky									
Lee Adjustment Ctr. (CCA)	644	1	0	3	1	4	0	3	0
Marion Adjustment Ctr. (CCA)	808	0	0	1	1	10	3	0	0
Louisiana									
Allen Corr. Ctr. (GEO)	1,457	1	0	0	0	0	0	0	0
Winn Corr. Ctr. (CCA)	1,458	2	0	0	0	2	1	1	0
Mississippi									
Delta Corr. Fac. (CCA)	1,015	1	0	1	0	0	0	0	0
East Mississippi Corr. Fac. (GEO)	1,332	2	1	0	0	0	0	0	0
Grenada Co. (MS DOC)	182	0	0	0	0	0	0	1	0
Walnut Grove Corr. Fac. (GEO)[c]	1,117	5	1	/	/	3	1	0	0
Wilkinson Co. Corr. Ctr. (CCA)	929	1	0	0	0	1	0	1	0
Montana									
Comm. Counseling & Corr. Svs., Inc. (CCCS)	190	1	0	0	0	0	0	0	0
Crossroads Corr. Ctr. (CCA)	625	4	0	0	0	5	0	1	0
WATCh East (CCCS)	106	1	0	0	0	0	0	0	0

TABLE 11 (continued)
Allegations of sexual victimization reported by privately operated jail and prison authorities, by type of victimization, 2010

Jurisdiction and facility	Average daily population	Inmate-on-inmate				Staff-on-inmate			
		Nonconsensual sexual acts		Abusive sexual contact		Sexual misconduct		Sexual harassment	
		Alleged	Substantiated	Alleged	Substantiated	Alleged	Substantiated	Alleged	Substantiated
New Mexico									
Cibola Co. Corr. Ctr. (CCA)[c]	1,156	0	0	/	/	0	0	1	0
Lea Co. Corr. Fac. (GEO)[c]	1,025	2	0	/	/	1	1	0	0
New Mexico Women's Corr. Fac. (CCA)[c]	603	1	0	/	/	2	0	0	0
Ohio									
Harbor Light (Salvation Army)[c]	171	0	0	/	/	3	0	2	1
Lake Erie Corr. Inst. (MTC)	1,495	0	0	1	0	0	0	0	0
Northeast Ohio Corr. Ctr. (CCA)	2,024	1	0	1	0	4	0	1	0
Oklahoma									
Cimarron Corr. Fac. (CCA)	649	1	0	1	0	2	0	4	0
David L. Moss Criminal Justice Ctr. (Tulsa Co., CCA)	1,548	1	0	3	0	1	0	0	0
Davis Corr. Fac. (CCA)	1,589	4	1	2	1	2	0	0	0
Lawton Corr. Fac. (GEO)	2,477	16	4	8	0	5	2	0	0
Pennsylvania									
George W. Hill Corr. Fac. (CEC)[c]	1,699	2	0	/	/	0	0	3	1
Tennessee									
Hardeman Co. (CCA)	1,966	6	0	5	1	5	0	0	0
Silverdale Corr. Fac. (CCA)	913	2	0	5	0	2	0	1	0
South Central Corr. Ctr. (CCA)	1,627	7	0	0	0	2	0	0	0
West Tennessee Det. Fac. (CCA)	549	1	0	1	0	2	0	3	0
Whiteville Corr. Fac. (CCA)[e]	1,492	1	0	2	0	5	0	4	1
Texas									
Big Spring Corr. Ctr. (GEO)[c]	3,485	0	0	/	/	0	0	1	0
Dalby Corr. Ctr. (MTC)	1,900	0	0	0	0	3	0	0	0
Eden Corr. Ctr. (CCA)	1,537	0	0	0	0	2	0	0	0
Houston-Reid Ctr. (GEO)	495	0	0	1	0	0	0	0	0
Val Verde Corr. Fac. & Co. Jail	1,275	1	0	1	0	0	0	0	0
Virginia									
Lawrenceville Corr. Ctr. (GEO)	1,574	1	0	1	0	1	0	0	0
Wyoming									
Campbell Co. Corr. Fac. (VOA)	105	0	0	0	0	0	0	2	0

CCA - Corrections Corp. of America

CCCS - Community Counseling & Corr. Services, Inc.

CEC - Community Education Centers, Inc.

DC - Dismas Charities (operates as Diersen Charities in New Mexico and Tennessee)

DOC - Department of Corrections

GEO - The GEO Group, Inc.

MTC - Management & Training Corp.

VOA - Volunteers of America

/ Not reported.

[a]Allegations of staff sexual harassment could not be counted separately from allegations of staff sexual misconduct.

[b]Counts of nonconsensual sexual acts were based on substantiated allegations only.

[c]Allegations of abusive sexual contact could not be counted separately from allegations of nonconsensual sexual acts.

[d]Average daily population was imputed.

[e]Counts of staff sexual misconduct were based on substantiated allegations only.

Source: Bureau of Justice Statistics, Survey of Sexual Violence, 2010.

TABLE 12
Allegations of sexual victimization reported by privately operated jail and prison authorities, by type of victimization, 2009

Jurisdiction and facility	Average daily population	Inmate-on-inmate				Staff-on-inmate			
		Nonconsensual sexual acts		Abusive sexual contact		Sexual misconduct		Sexual harassment	
		Alleged	Substantiated	Alleged	Substantiated	Alleged	Substantiated	Alleged	Substantiated
Total	68,465	91	3	38	4	90	24	22	1
Arizona									
Arizona State Prison - Kingman (MTC)[a]	1,460	0	0	0	0	1	1	/	/
Eloy Det. Ctr. (CCA)	1,514	0	0	1	0	2	2	0	0
California									
California City Corr. Ctr. (CCA)	2,583	5	0	0	0	0	0	0	0
Colorado									
Bent Co. Corr. Fac. (CCA)	1,388	1	0	1	0	1	1	0	0
Cheyenne Mountain Reentry Ctr. (CEC)	723	0	0	3	1	1	1	0	0
Crowley Co. Corr. Fac. (CCA)	1,420	0	0	0	0	4	1	0	0
Kit Carson Co. Corr. Ctr. (CCA)	1,324	1	0	1	0	0	0	0	0
Phoenix Ctr. Adams Co. Comm. Corr. (CEC)[a,b,c,d]	218	0	0	/	/	2	0	/	/
Florida									
Bay Corr. Inst. (CCA)	981	0	0	0	0	2	0	0	0
Gadsden Corr. Fac. (CCA)	1,511	1	0	2	0	4	0	1	0
Hernando Co. (CCA)	706	1	0	0	0	0	0	0	0
South Bay Corr. Fac. (GEO)[c]	1,854	1	0	/	/	0	0	0	0
Georgia									
Coffee Corr. Fac. (CCA)	1,685	2	0	0	0	0	0	0	0
D. Ray James Prison (GEO)	1,798	4	0	0	0	9	0	5	0
McRae Corr. Fac. (CCA)	1,735	0	0	0	0	2	1	0	0
Wheeler Corr. Fac. (CCA)[c]	1,688	3	0	/	/	0	0	0	0
Indiana									
Marion Co. Jail II (CCA)	1,135	0	0	6	0	0	0	1	0
Kentucky									
Lee Adjustment Ctr. (CCA)	696	6	1	2	1	4	1	1	0
Marion Adjustment Ctr. (CCA)	815	0	0	3	0	5	0	0	0
Otter Creek Corr. Complex (CCA)[c]	429	2	0	/	/	7	2	2	0
Louisiana									
Allen Corr. Ctr. (GEO)	1,459	3	1	0	0	1	1	0	0
Winn Corr. Ctr. (CCA)	1,461	3	0	0	0	0	0	7	1
Mississippi									
Delta Corr. Fac. (CCA)	949	0	0	0	0	0	0	1	0
East Mississippi Corr. Fac. (GEO)	1,350	3	0	3	0	1	1	0	0
Walnut Grove Corr. Fac. (GEO)	1,203	7	0	0	0	0	0	0	0
Wilkinson Co. Corr. Ctr. (CCA)	971	1	0	0	0	0	0	0	0
Montana									
Alpha House (Alternatives, Inc.)	196	1	0	0	0	1	0	0	0
Crossroads Corr. Ctr. (CCA)	621	1	0	1	0	0	0	0	0
New Mexico									
Guadalupe Co. Corr. Fac. (GEO)	550	0	0	0	0	1	1	0	0
New Mexico Women's Corr. Fac. (CCA)	585	2	0	1	0	7	1	0	0
North Carolina									
Rivers Corr. Inst. (GEO)	1,345	2	0	0	0	0	0	0	0
Ohio									
Lake Erie Corr. Inst. (MTC)	1,488	2	0	0	0	0	0	0	0
North Coast Corr. Treatment Fac. (MTC)[c]	690	1	0	/	/	0	0	0	0
Northeast Ohio Corr. Ctr. (CCA)	2,019	0	0	0	0	1	0	0	0
Oriana House, Inc.	19	0	0	3	0	1	0	0	0

TABLE 12 (continued)
Allegations of sexual victimization reported by privately operated jail and prison authorities, by type of victimization, 2009

Jurisdiction and facility	Average daily population	Inmate-on-inmate				Staff-on-inmate			
		Nonconsensual sexual acts		Abusive sexual contact		Sexual misconduct		Sexual harassment	
		Alleged	Substantiated	Alleged	Substantiated	Alleged	Substantiated	Alleged	Substantiated
Oklahoma									
Cimarron Corr. Fac. (CCA)	931	3	0	0	0	4	1	1	0
David L. Moss Criminal Justice Ctr. (Tulsa Co., CCA)	1,600	0	0	2	1	0	0	0	0
Davis Corr. Fac. (CCA)	1,265	4	0	0	0	3	3	0	0
Diamondback Corr. Fac. (CCA)	2,104	1	0	0	0	1	0	0	0
Lawton Corr. Fac. (GEO)[a,c]	2,496	15	1	/	/	4	2	/	/
Pennsylvania									
Capitol Pavilion Comm. Corr. Ctr. (CEC)[a]	93	0	0	0	0	2	0	/	/
George W. Hill Corr. Fac. (CEC)	1,925	0	0	0	0	1	0	0	0
Tennessee									
Dismas House - Nashville (DC)	62	0	0	0	0	1	1	0	0
Hardeman Co. (CCA)	1,964	4	0	1	0	2	0	1	0
Metro-Davidson Co. Det. Fac. (CCA)	1,103	1	0	3	0	2	0	0	0
West Tennessee Det. Fac. (CCA)	574	1	0	2	0	0	0	0	0
Whiteville Corr. Fac. (CCA)	1,487	3	0	0	0	4	3	0	0
Texas									
Dalby Corr. Ctr. (MTC)	1,864	1	0	0	0	4	0	0	0
Dawson State Jail (CCA)[a,c]	2,195	1	0	/	/	1	0	/	/
Eden Corr. Ctr. (CCA)	1,541	0	0	0	0	1	0	0	0
Houston-Reid Ctr. (GEO)	452	1	0	1	0	0	0	0	0
Lindsey State Jail (CCA)	1,027	0	0	1	1	0	0	0	0
Lockhart Prison Work Program (GEO)	991	1	0	1	0	0	0	0	0
Reeves Co. Det. Complex R1, R2, & R3 (GEO)	1,342	/	/	0	0	1	0	0	0
Val Verde Corr. Fac. & Co. Jail	1,251	1	0	0	0	0	0	0	0
Virginia									
Lawrenceville Corr. Ctr. (GEO)	1,566	1	0	0	0	1	0	2	0
Washington									
Bishop Lewis House Work Release (Pioneer Human Svs.)[c]	63	0	0	/	/	1	0	0	0

CCA - Corrections Corp. of America

CEC - Community Education Centers, Inc.

DC - Dismas Charities (operates as Diersen Charities in New Mexico and Tennessee)

GEO - The GEO Group, Inc.

MTC - Management & Training Corp

/ Not reported.

[a]Allegations of staff sexual harassment could not be counted separately from allegations of staff sexual misconduct.

[b]Counts of nonconsensual sexual acts were based on substantiated allegations only.

[c]Allegations of abusive sexual contact could not be counted separately from allegations of nonconsensual sexual acts.

[d]Counts of staff sexual misconduct were based on substantiated allegations only.

Source: Bureau of Justice Statistics, Survey of Sexual Violence, 2009.

TABLE 13
Privately operated jail and prison authorities with no allegations of sexual victimization, 2011

Jurisdiction and facility	Average daily population	Jurisdiction and facility	Average daily population
Total	30,854	**New Mexico**	
Alaska		Valencia Co. Det. Ctr.	163
Seaside Ctr. (GEO)	41	**North Carolina**	
Arizona		Salvation Army (CCC)[a,b]	36
Marana Comm. Corr. Treatment Fac.	494	**Ohio**	
California		Canton Comm. Treatment & Corr. Ctr.	44
Golden State Modified Comm. Corr. Fac. (GEO)[a]	567	Columbiana Co. (CEC)	121
La Cienega Work Furlough Program (VOA)	50	Comm. Corr. Assn., Inc.	153
Colorado		Mansfield Corr. Program (VOA)	120
Arapahoe Comm. Treatment Ctr.	138	North Coast Corr. Treatment Fac. (MTC)	690
Centennial Comm. Transition Ctr.	101	**Oklahoma**	
Corr. Alternatives Placement Svs.	30	Avalon Corr. Ctr. (Avalon Corr. Svs., Inc.)[a,b]	247
Intervention Comm. Corr. Svs. - Lakewood[a,b]	230	Ctr. Point, Inc.[a,b]	154
Connecticut		**South Dakota**	
Sierra Ctr. Work Release (The Connection)	26	Comm. Alcohol Drug Ctr., Stepping Stone	17
Watkinson House	39	**Tennessee**	
District of Columbia		Dismas House - Nashville (DC)[a,b]	52
Hope Village (CCC)	277	**Texas**	
Florida		Bartlett State Jail (CCA)	1,044
Bridges of Pompano - Turning Point W.R.C. (BOA)	206	Big Spring Corr. Ctr. (GEO)[a]	3,493
Broward Transitional Ctr. (GEO)	629	Billy M. Moore Corr. Ctr. (MTC)	499
Comm. Corr. Ctr. (Spectrum Programs, Inc.)	72	Bradshaw State Jail (CCA)	1,963
Moore Haven Corr. Fac. (CCA)	978	Bridgeport Corr. Fac. (GEO, CCA)	520
Pompano Transit Ctr., Male (FL DOC)	180	Bridgeport PPT (CCA)	199
The Salvation Army	56	Cleveland Corr. Ctr. (GEO)	519
Illinois		Crosspoint, Inc.	115
Crossroads Adult Transitional Ctr.[a]	325	Dawson State Jail (CCA)	2,199
North Lawndale Adult Transition Ctr. (Safer Foundation)	197	Diboll Unit (MTC)	518
Substance Abuse Svs. (The H Group)	52	Estes Corr. Ctr. (MTC)	1,038
Indiana		Kyle Corr. Ctr. (MTC)	519
Marion Co. Jail II (CCA)	1,033	Limestone Co. (CEC)[a]	749
Kansas		Lindsey State Jail (CCA)	1,026
Grossman Ctr. (GEO)	90	Lockhart Prison Work Program (GEO)	498
Kentucky		Mineral Wells PPT (CCA)	2,058
Paducah Comm. Svs. Ctr.	85	Willacy Co. State Jail (CCA)	1,068
York Street House (Transitions, Inc.)	9	**Utah**	
Louisiana		Salt Lake City Reentry Ctr. (GEO)	110
Catahoula Corr. Ctr. (LaSalle Southwest Corr.)	812		
St. Martin DePorres Res. Ctr. (Cinc Inc.)	170		
Maryland			
Threshold, Inc.	30		
Michigan			
Monica House (CTC)	54		
Mississippi			
East Mississippi Corr. Fac. (GEO)	1,332		
Missouri			
Dismas House - St. Louis (DC)	180		
Montana			
Comm. Counseling & Corr. Svs., Inc. (CCCS)	178		
Great Falls Pre-Release Svs., Inc.	241		
New Jersey			
Bo Robinson Assessment & Treatment Ctr. (EHCA & CEC)[a]	693		
Kintock	432		
Millicent Fenwick House (NJAC)	49		
Talbot Hall (EHCA & CEC)	510		
Tully House (EHCA & CEC)	336		

CCA - Corrections Corp. of America

CCCS - Community Counseling & Corr. Services, Inc.

CEC - Community Education Centers, Inc.

DC - Dismas Charities (operates as Diersen Charities in New Mexico and Tennessee)

DOC - Department of Corrections

EHCA - Education & Health Centers of America

GEO - The GEO Group, Inc.

MTC - Management & Training Corp.

VOA - Volunteers of America

[a]Allegations of abusive sexual contact could not be counted separately from allegations of nonconsensual sexual acts.

[b]Allegations of staff sexual harassment could not be counted separately from allegations of staff sexual misconduct.

Source: Bureau of Justice Statistics, Survey of Sexual Violence, 2011.

TABLE 14
Privately operated jail and prison authorities with no allegations of sexual victimization, 2010

Jurisdiction and facility	Average daily population	Jurisdiction and facility	Average daily population
Total	37,966	North Dakota	
Alaska		Bismarck Transition Ctr. (CCCS)	131
Glacier Manor (Gastineau Human Svs.)	86	Ohio	
Arizona		Comm. Assessment & Training Svs., Inc.	104
Arizona State Prison - Florence West (GEO)[a]	736	Comm. Corr. Assn., Inc.	72
Arizona State Prison - Phoenix West (GEO)	493	North Coast Corr. Treatment Fac. (MTC)	690
Marana Comm. Corr. Treatment Fac.	490	Northwest Ohio (VOA)[e]	73
Tuscon Res. Reentry Ctr. (Behavioral Systems Southwest)[a,b]	53	Oklahoma	
California		Avalon Corr. Ctr. (Avalon Corr. Svs., Inc.)	250
Central Valley Modified Comm. Corr. Fac. (GEO)	606	Bridgeway Inc.	103
Golden State Modified Comm. Corr. Fac. (GEO)	603	Pennsylvania	
Taft Corr. Inst. (MTC)	2,342	Alle Kiski Pavillion (CEC)	82
Colorado		Allegheny Co. Reentry Program (Renewal, Inc.)	550
Arapahoe Co. Res. Ctr. (CEC)[a,b]	139	Texas	
Pueblo Comm. Corr. Svs., Inc.	80	Bartlett State Jail (CCA)[a,b]	1,045
The Phoenix Ctr. (CEC)	214	Billy M. Moore Corr. Ctr. (MTC)[a]	499
Connecticut		Bradshaw State Jail (CCA)[a,b]	1,966
Morris Therapeutic Shelter (Wellmore Behavioral Health)[a,b]	21	Bridgeport Corr. Fac. (GEO, CCA)[a,b]	519
Roger Sherman House (The Connection)	55	Bridgeport PPT (CCA)[a,b]	200
District of Columbia		Cleveland Corr. Ctr. (GEO)[a,b]	519
Hope Village (CCC)[a,b]	314	Crystal City Corr. Ctr. (LaSalle Southwest Corr.)	411
Florida		Dawson State Jail (CCA)[a,b]	2,194
Bay Co. (CCA)	885	Diboll Unit (MTC)[a,b]	517
Hillsborough Co. Res. Reentry Ctr. (Goodwill Ind.-Suncoast, Inc.)	93	Estes Corr. Ctr. (MTC)[a,b]	1,038
Lake City Corr. Fac. (CCA)	887	Kyle Corr. Ctr. (MTC)[a,b]	459
Moore Haven Corr. Fac. (GEO, CCA)[a,b,c]	979	Limestone Co. (CEC)[a,b]	766
Pompano Transit Ctr., male (FL DOC)	212	Lindsey State Jail (CCA)[a,b]	1,028
Reentry of Ocala Work Release Ctr., male (Time for Freedom, Inc.)	129	Lockhart Prison Work Program (GEO)[a,b]	498
Illinois		Midvalley House (GEO)	139
North Lawndale Adult Transition Ctr. (Safer Foundation)[c]	197	Mineral Wells PPT (CCA)[a,b]	2,061
Kentucky		Reeves Co., Complex 2 (GEO)	1,910
Portland - Louisville (DC)	216	Reeves Co., Det. Complex R1, R2, & R3 (GEO)	1,335
Two Rivers Treatment Ctr. (Transitions, Inc.)	60	Willacy Co. State Jail (CCA)[a,b]	1,069
Louisiana		Wisconsin	
St. Martin DePorres Res. Ctr. (Cinc, Inc.)	213	Alternative Program (Rock Valley Comm. Programs Inc.)[e]	66
Minnesota			
Bethel Work Release Program (The Duluth Bethel)[a,b]	53		
Mississippi			
Marshall Co. Corr. Fac. (GEO)[a,b]	907		
Tallahatchie Co. Corr. Fac. (CCA)[d]	2,622		
New Jersey			
Field House (VOA)	29		
Kintock	432		
Talbot Hall (EHCA & CEC)	507		
Tully House (EHCA & CEC)[a,b]	305		
New Mexico			
Dismas House - Albuquerque (DC)	47		
Guadalupe Co. Corr. Fac. (GEO)	557		
Lincoln Co. Det. Ctr. (NM Sentencing Commission)[b]	128		
Santa Fe Co.	450		
New York			
Bronx Comm. Reentry Ctr. (GEO)	117		
North Carolina			
Dismas House - Greensboro (DC)	66		
Rivers Corr. Inst. (GEO)[a,b]	1,349		

CCA - Corrections Corp. of America

CCCS - Community Counseling & Corr. Services, Inc.

CEC - Community Education Centers, Inc.

DC - Dismas Charities (operates as Diersen Charities in New Mexico and Tennessee)

DOC - Department of Corrections

EHCA - Education & Health Centers of America

GEO - The GEO Group, Inc.

MTC - Management & Training Corp.

VOA - Volunteers of America

[a]Allegations of staff sexual harassment could not be counted separately from allegations of staff sexual misconduct.

[b]Allegations of abusive sexual contact could not be counted separately from allegations of nonconsensual sexual acts.

[c]Average daily population was imputed.

[d]Counts of nonconsensual sexual acts were based on completed acts only.

[e]Counts of staff sexual misconduct were based on substantiated allegations only.

Source: Bureau of Justice Statistics, Survey of Sexual Violence, 2010.

TABLE 15
Privately operated jail and prison authorities with no allegations of sexual victimization, 2009

Jurisdiction and facility	Average daily population	Jurisdiction and facility	Average daily population
Total	41,837	**New Mexico**	
Alaska		Cibola Co. Corr. Ctr. (CCA)	1,146
Parkview Ctr. (GEO)[a,b]	112	Lea Co. Corr. Fac. (GEO)[a,b]	1,226
Arizona		Torrance Co. Det. Fac. (CCA)	688
Arizona State Prison - Florence West (GEO)	741	**New York**	
Arizona State Prison - Phoenix West (GEO)[a]	496	Brooklyn Comm. Corr. Ctr. (GEO)[a,b]	175
Marana Comm. Corr. Treatment Fac.	474	**North Carolina**	
Arkansas		The Ctr. for Comm. Transitions (ECO)[b]	20
City of Faith Comm. Corr. Ctr.	76	**Ohio**	
California		Cliff Skeen CBCF for Women (Oriana House, Inc.)	19
Alhambra City Jail (GEO)[a,b]	6	Mansfield Corr. Program (VOA)	67
Central Valley Modified Comm. Corr. Fac. (GEO)	600	**Oklahoma**	
Corr. Alternatives, Inc.[a,b]	233	Avalon Corr. Ctr. (Avalon Corr. Svs., Inc.)[a,b]	250
Desert View Modified Comm. Corr. Fac. (GEO)	628	Ctr. Point, Inc.	170
Golden State Modified Comm. Corr. Fac. (GEO)	580	Great Plains Corr. Fac. (CCI)	1,889
National Crossroads[a,b]	65	**Tennessee**	
Taft Corr. Inst. (MTC)	2,340	South Central Corr. Ctr. (CCA)	1,625
Colorado		**Texas**	
Centennial Comm. Transition Ctr.[a,b]	89	Bartlett State Jail (CCA)	1,046
ComCor Women's Fac. (ComCor, Inc.)[a]	328	Big Spring Corr. Ctr. (GEO)	3,471
Independence House - Fillmore	41	Billy M. Moore Corr. Ctr. (MTC)	499
Independence House - South Federal	90	Bradshaw State Jail (CCA)	1,968
Intervention Comm. Corr. Svs. - Lakewood[a,b,c]	245	Bridgeport Corr. Fac. (GEO, CCA)	519
Connecticut		Cleveland Corr. Ctr. (GEO)	519
Next Step	15	Crystal City Corr. Ctr. (LaSalle Southwest Corr.)	435
Florida		Diboll Unit (MTC)	518
Bridges of Pompano - Turning Point WRC. (BOA)[a,b]	195	Estes Corr. Ctr. (MTC)[c]	1,038
Broward Transitional Ctr. (GEO)	530	Frio Co. (GEO)	334
Lake City Corr. Fac. (CCA)[a]	897	Kyle Corr. Ctr. (MTC)	480
Moore Haven Corr. Fac. (GEO)	980	Leidel Comprehensive Sanction Ctr. (GEO)	218
Reality House[a,b]	128	Limestone Co. (CEC)	744
Salvation Army Red Shield Lodge	57	McCabe Ctr. (GEO)	110
Illinois		Mineral Wells PPT (CCA)	2,036
Cornell Interventions Southwood (CCI)	91	Reeves Co., Complex 2 (GEO)[a,b]	1,763
Kansas		Rolling Plains Corr. Fac. (Emerald Companies)	518
Grossman Ctr. (CCI)	95	Willacy Co. State Jail (CCA)	1,068
Kentucky		**Wyoming**	
Portland - Louisville (DC)[a,b]	220	Comm. Alternatives of Casper & Reentry Ctr. (CEC)	295
St. Ann's - Louisville (DC)[a]	66		
Louisiana			
Catahoula Corr. Ctr. (LaSalle Southwest Corr.)[d]	827		
Michigan			
Monica House (CTC)	55		
Minnesota			
Prairie Corr. Fac. (CCA)	191		
Mississippi			
Marshall Co. Corr. Fac. (GEO)	975		
Tallahatchie Co. Corr. Fac. (CCA)	2,572		
Nevada			
Las Vegas Comm. Corr. Ctr. (CCI)	126		
New Jersey			
Bo Robinson Assessment & Treatment Ctr. (EHCA & CEC)[a,b]	533		
Garrett House (VOA)	40		
Hope Hall (VOA)	165		
Kintock	615		
Talbot Hall (EHCA & CEC)	466		

CCA - Corrections Corp. of America
CCCS - Community Counseling & Corr. Services, Inc.
CCI - Cornell Companies, Inc.
CEC - Community Education Centers, Inc.
DC - Dismas Charities (operates as Diersen Charities in New Mexico and Tennessee)
DOC - Department of Corrections
EHCA - Education & Health Centers of America
GEO - The GEO Group, Inc.
MTC - Management & Training Corp.
VOA - Volunteers of America

[a]Allegations of abusive sexual contact could not be counted separately from allegations of nonconsensual sexual acts.
[b]Allegations of staff sexual harassment could not be counted separately from allegations of staff sexual misconduct.
[c]Counts of staff sexual misconduct were based on substantiated allegations only.
[d]Counts of nonconsensual sexual acts were based on substantiated allegations only.
Source: Bureau of Justice Statistics, Survey of Sexual Violence, 2009.

Section 4. Other correctional facilities: U.S. military, U.S. Immigration and Customs Enforcement, and Jails in Indian Country

TABLE 16

Allegations of sexual victimization reported by other correctional facility authorities, by type of victimization, 2011

| | | Inmate-on-inmate | | | | Staff-on-inmate | | | |
| | Average daily population | Nonconsensual sexual acts | | Abusive sexual contact | | Sexual misconduct | | Sexual harassment | |
Jurisdiction and facility		Alleged	Substantiated	Alleged	Substantiated	Alleged	Substantiated	Alleged	Substantiated
Total	16,996	6	1	29	7	18	1	4	0
U.S. military									
Total	1,524	0	0	3	2	1	0	0	0
Office of Legal Policy - Air Force	49	0	0	0	0	0	0	0	0
Office of Legal Policy - Army	780	0	0	0	0	0	0	0	0
Office of Legal Policy - Marines	140	0	0	0	0	0	0	0	0
Office of Legal Policy - Navy	555	0	0	3	2	1	0	0	0
U.S. Immigration and Customs Enforcement (ICE)									
Total	14,669	6	1	25	4	16	0	3	0
Arizona									
ICE - Florence Svs. Processing Ctr.	342	1	1	0	0	0	0	0	0
California									
ICE - El Centro Svs. Processing Ctr.[a,b]	480	0	0	/	/	0	0	/	/
ICE - Mira Loma Det. Ctr.	1,039	0	0	0	0	1	0	0	0
ICE - San Diego Otay Det. Fac.	1,035	2	0	3	0	6	0	3	0
Colorado									
ICE - Denver Contract Det. Fac.[a,b]	408	0	0	/	/	0	0	/	/
Florida									
ICE - Broward Transitional Ctr. (GEO)	629	0	0	0	0	0	0	0	0
ICE - Krome Svs. Processing Ctr.	604	0	0	9	0	1	0	0	0
Georgia									
ICE - Stewart Det. Ctr.	1,652	0	0	3	0	0	0	0	0
Louisiana									
ICE - LaSalle Det. Fac.	946	0	0	0	0	0	0	0	0
New Jersey									
ICE - Elizabeth Contract Det. Fac.	265	1	0	3	1	1	0	0	0
New York									
ICE - Buffalo Fed. Det. Fac.	617	0	0	0	0	0	0	0	0
Texas									
ICE - El Paso Svs. Processing Ctr.	640	0	0	1	0	3	0	0	0
ICE - Houston Contract Det. Fac.	875	0	0	2	0	3	0	0	0
ICE - Laredo Contract Det. Fac.	267	0	0	0	0	0	0	0	0
ICE - Otero Co. Processing Ctr.	866	0	0	0	0	0	0	0	0
ICE - Port Isabel Svs. Processing Ctr.	1,164	1	0	1	0	0	0	0	0
ICE - South Texas Det. Complex[a,b]	1,665	0	0	/	/	1	0	/	/
Washington									
ICE - Tacoma Contract Det. Fac.	1,175	1	0	3	3	0	0	0	0
Jails in Indian country									
Total	803	0	0	1	1	1	1	1	0
Arizona									
Colorado River Indian Tribes Adult Det.[a,b]	60	0	0	/	/	0	0	/	/
Gila River Dept. of Rehab. & Supervision - Adult	133	0	0	0	0	0	0	1	0
Navajo Dept. of Corr. - Kayenta[a,b]	9	0	0	/	/	0	0	/	/
San Carlos Dept. of Corr. & Rehab. - Adult & Juv. Det.	140	0	0	0	0	0	0	0	0

TABLE 16 (continued)
Allegations of sexual victimization reported by other correctional facility authorities, by type of victimization, 2011

Jurisdiction and facility	Average daily population	Inmate-on-inmate				Staff-on-inmate			
		Nonconsensual sexual acts		Abusive sexual contact		Sexual misconduct		Sexual harassment	
		Alleged	Substantiated	Alleged	Substantiated	Alleged	Substantiated	Alleged [a,b]	Substantiated
Arizona (continued)									
Tohono O'odham Adult Det. Ctr.[a,b]	180	0	0	/	/	0	0	0	0
White Mountain Apache Det. Ctr.	77	0	0	0	0	0	0	0	0
Idaho									
Fort Hall P.D. & Adult Det.	45	0	0	0	0	0	0	0	0
Nevada									
Eastern Nevada L.E. Adult Det.	18	0	0	0	0	0	0	0	0
New Mexico									
Jicarilla Dept. of Corr., Adult & Juv.	30	0	0	0	0	0	0	0	0
South Dakota									
Rosebud Sioux Tribal P.D. & Adult Det.	56	0	0	1	1	1	1	0	0
Washington									
Spokane Adult Det. Ctr.[a]	5	0	0	/	/	0	0	0	0
Wisconsin									
Menominee Tribal Det. Fac.[c,d]	50	0	0	/	/	0	0	/	/

/ Not reported.

[a]Allegations of abusive sexual contact could not be counted separately from allegations of nonconsensual sexual acts.

[b]Allegations of staff sexual harassment could not be counted separately from allegations of staff sexual misconduct.

[c]Agency did not record allegations of abusive sexual contact.

[d]Agency did not record allegations of staff sexual harassment.

Source: Bureau of Justice Statistics, Survey of Sexual Violence, 2011.

TABLE 17

Allegations of sexual victimization reported by other correctional facility authorities, by type of victimization, 2010

| Jurisdiction and facility | Average daily population | Inmate-on-inmate | | | | Staff-on-inmate | | | |
| | | Nonconsensual sexual acts | | Abusive sexual contact | | Sexual misconduct | | Sexual harassment | |
		Alleged	Substantiated	Alleged	Substantiated	Alleged	Substantiated	Alleged	Substantiated
Total	19,551	11	1	19	1	11	2	12	1
U.S. military									
Total	1,520	2	0	3	1	1	1	0	0
Office of Legal Policy - Air Force	46	0	0	0	0	0	0	0	0
Office of Legal Policy - Army	714	1	0	1	0	0	0	0	0
Office of Legal Policy - Marines	287	0	0	0	0	0	0	0	0
Office of Legal Policy - Navy	473	1	0	2	1	1	1	0	0
U.S. Immigration and Customs Enforcement (ICE)									
Total	17,318	8	0	16	0	10	1	12	1
Arizona									
ICE - Florence Svs. Processing Ctr.	1,613	2	0	0	0	1	0	0	0
California									
ICE - El Centro Svs. Processing Ctr.[a]	455	0	0	0	0	0	0	/	/
ICE - Mira Loma Det. Ctr.	1,201	0	0	0	0	0	0	0	0
ICE - San Diego Otay Det. Fac.	1,042	4	0	4	0	0	0	8	0
Colorado									
ICE - Denver Contract Det. Fac.	415	0	0	0	0	0	0	0	0
Florida									
ICE - Broward Transitional Ctr. (GEO)	601	0	0	0	0	0	0	0	0
ICE - Krome Svs. Processing Ctr.	541	0	0	0	0	0	0	0	0
Georgia									
ICE - Stewart Det. Ctr.	1,700	0	0	1	0	1	0	2	0
Louisiana									
ICE - LaSalle Det. Fac.	923	0	0	0	0	1	1	0	0
New Jersey									
ICE - Elizabeth Contract Det. Fac.	246	0	0	0	0	1	0	0	0
New York									
ICE - Buffalo Fed. Det. Fac.	606	0	0	0	0	0	0	0	0
Texas									
ICE - El Paso Svs. Processing Ctr.	791	0	0	7	0	5	0	0	0
ICE - Houston Contract Det. Fac.	868	0	0	3	0	1	0	1	1
ICE - Laredo Contract Det. Fac.	214	0	0	0	0	0	0	0	0
ICE - Otero Co. Processing Ctr.[a,b]	1,255	0	0	/	/	0	0	/	/
ICE - Port Isabel Svs. Processing Ctr.	885	1	0	1	0	0	0	0	0
ICE - South Texas Det. Complex[a,b]	1,499	1	0	/	/	0	0	/	/
ICE - Willacy Det. Ctr.	1,255	0	0	0	0	0	0	1	0
Washington									
ICE - Tacoma Contract Det. Fac.	1,208	0	0	0	0	0	0	0	0
Jails in Indian country									
Total	713	1	1	0	0	0	0	0	0
Arizona									
Gila River Dept. of Rehab. & Supervision Adult[a,b]	110	0	0	/	/	0	0	/	/
Navajo Dept. of Corr. - Tuba City[c]	14	0	0	0	0	0	0	0	0
Navajo Dept. of Corr. - Window Rock	25	0	0	0	0	0	0	0	0
San Carlos Dept. of Corr. & Rehab - Adult & Juv. Det.	111	0	0	0	0	0	0	0	0
Tohono O'odham Adult Det. Ctr.[e,f,g]	180	0	0	/	/	/	/	/	/
Colorado									
Southern Ute P.D. & Adult Det.[a,b]	28	0	0	/	/	0	0	/	/

TABLE 17 (continued)

Allegations of sexual victimization reported by other correctional facility authorities, by type of victimization, 2010

Jurisdiction and facility	Average daily population	Inmate-on-inmate				Staff-on-inmate			
		Nonconsensual sexual acts		Abusive sexual contact		Sexual misconduct		Sexual harassment	
		Alleged	Substantiated	Alleged	Substantiated	Alleged	Substantiated	Alleged	Substantiated
Montana									
Blackfeet Adult Det. Ctr.	12	1	1	0	0	0	0	0	0
Nebraska									
Omaha Tribal P.D. & Adult Det.	25	0	0	0	0	0	0	0	0
New Mexico									
Laguna Tribal Police & Det. Ctr.	45	0	0	0	0	0	0	0	0
North Dakota									
Turtle Mountain L.E. Adult Det.	13	0	0	0	0	0	0	0	0
South Dakota									
Kyle P.D. & Adult Det.	26	0	0	0	0	0	0	0	0
Washington									
Nisqually Adult Corr.	70	0	0	0	0	0	0	0	0
Wisconsin									
Menominee Tribal Det. Fac.[b]	54	0	0	/	/	0	0	0	0

/ Not reported.

[a]Allegations of staff sexual harassment could not be counted separately from allegations of staff sexual misconduct.

[b]Allegations of abusive sexual contact could not be counted separately from allegations of nonconsensual sexual acts.

[c]Counts of nonconsensual sexual acts were based on substantiated allegations only.

[d]Agency did not record allegations of nonconsensual sexual acts.

[e]Agency did not record allegations of abusive sexual contact.

[f]Agency did not record allegations of staff sexual misconduct.

[g]Agency did not record allegations of staff sexual harassment.

Source: Bureau of Justice Statistics, Survey of Sexual Violence, 2010.

TABLE 18
Allegations of sexual victimization reported by other correctional facility authorities, by type of victimization, 2009

Jurisdiction and facility	Average daily population	Inmate-on-inmate				Staff-on-inmate			
		Nonconsensual sexual acts		Abusive sexual contact		Sexual misconduct		Sexual harassment	
		Alleged	Substantiated	Alleged	Substantiated	Alleged	Substantiated	Alleged	Substantiated
Total	16,947	5	1	4	2	8	1	1	0
U.S. military									
Total	1,595	1	0	0	0	0	0	0	0
Office of Legal Policy - Air Force	50	0	0	0	0	0	0	0	0
Office of Legal Policy - Army	665	0	0	0	0	0	0	0	0
Office of Legal Policy - Marines	384	0	0	0	0	0	0	0	0
Office of Legal Policy - Navy	496	1	0	0	0	0	0	0	0
U.S. Immigration and Customs Enforcement (ICE)									
Total	14,609	4	1	4	2	8	1	1	0
Arizona									
ICE - Florence Svs. Processing Ctr.[a]	848	0	0	/	/	1	0	0	0
California									
ICE - El Centro Svs. Processing Ctr.	480	0	0	0	0	0	0	0	0
ICE - Mira Loma Det. Ctr.[a]	1,000	0	0	/	/	0	0	0	0
ICE - San Diego Otay Det. Fac.	985	3	1	3	2	5	0	0	0
Colorado									
ICE - Denver Contract Det. Fac.	387	0	0	1	0	0	0	0	0
Florida									
ICE - Broward Transitional Ctr. (GEO)	536	0	0	0	0	0	0	0	0
ICE - Krome Svs. Processing Ctr.[a,b]	587	1	0	/	/	0	0	/	/
Georgia									
ICE - Stewart Det. Ctr.	1,622	0	0	0	0	0	0	0	0
Louisiana									
ICE - LaSalle Det. Fac.	408	0	0	0	0	1	1	0	0
New Jersey									
ICE - Elizabeth Contract Det. Fac.	215	0	0	0	0	0	0	0	0
New York									
ICE - Buffalo Fed. Det. Fac.	620	0	0	0	0	0	0	1	0
Texas									
ICE - El Paso Svs. Processing Ctr.	760	0	0	0	0	1	0	0	0
ICE - Houston Contract Det. Fac.	874	0	0	0	0	0	0	0	0
ICE - Laredo Contract Det. Fac.	267	0	0	0	0	0	0	0	0
ICE - Otero Co. Processing Ctr.[a,b]	842	0	0	/	/	0	0	/	/
ICE - Port Isabel Svs. Processing Ctr.	663	0	0	0	0	0	0	0	0
ICE - South Texas Det. Complex	1,584	0	0	0	0	0	0	0	0
ICE - Willacy Det. Ctr.	1,000	0	0	0	0	0	0	0	0
Washington									
ICE - Tacoma Contract Det. Fac.	931	0	0	0	0	0	0	0	0
Jails in Indian country									
Total	743	0	0	0	0	0	0	0	0
Arizona									
Colorado River Indian Tribes Adult Det.[c]	67	0	0	0	0	0	0	0	0
Gila River Dept. of Rehab. & Supervision Adult	121	0	0	0	0	0	0	0	0
Navajo Dept. of Corr. - Chinle	20	0	0	0	0	0	0	0	0
Salt River Pima-Maricopa Dept. of Corr.	30	0	0	0	0	0	0	0	0
San Carlos Dept. of Corr. & Rehab. - Adult & Juv. Det.	118	0	0	0	0	0	0	0	0
Tohono O'odham Adult Det. Ctr.	173	0	0	0	0	0	0	0	0
Colorado									
Southern Ute P.D. & Adult Det.	39	0	0	0	0	0	0	0	0

TABLE 18 (continued)
Allegations of sexual victimization reported by other correctional facility authorities, by type of victimization, 2009

| | | Inmate-on-inmate | | | | Staff-on-inmate | | | |
| | Average daily population | Nonconsensual sexual acts | | Abusive sexual contact | | Sexual misconduct | | Sexual harassment | |
Jurisdiction and facility		Alleged	Substantiated	Alleged	Substantiated	Alleged	Substantiated	Alleged	Substantiated
Nevada									
Eastern Nevada L.E. Adult Det.[a,b]	11	0	0	/	/	0	0	/	/
New Mexico									
Acoma Tribal Police & Holding Fac.	9	0	0	0	0	0	0	0	0
North Dakota									
Fort Totten L.E. & Adult Det. Ctr.	45	0	0	0	0	0	0	0	0
South Dakota									
Lower Brule Justice Ctr., Adult Det.	31	0	0	0	0	0	0	0	0
Washington									
Colville Adult Det. Ctr.	26	0	0	0	0	0	0	0	0
Wisconsin									
Menominee Tribal Det. Fac.[a,d]	53	0	0	/	/	0	0	0	0

/ Not reported.

[a]Allegations of abusive sexual contact could not be counted separately from allegations of nonconsensual sexual acts.

[b]Allegations of staff sexual harassment could not be counted separately from allegations of staff sexual misconduct.

[c]Agency did not record allegations of nonconsensual sexual acts.

[d]Counts of nonconsensual sexual acts were based on substantiated allegations only.

Source: Bureau of Justice Statistics, Survey of Sexual Violence, 2009.